THE other AMERICA

HOMELESS Teens

These and other titles are included in *The Other America* series:

THEotherAMERICA

HOMELESS Teens

by
Gail B. Stewart

Photographs by
Carl Franzén

Lucent Books, P.O. Box 289011, San Diego, CA 92198-9011

Cover design: Carl Franzén

Library of Congress Cataloging-in-Publication Data
Stewart, Gail B. 1949–
    Homeless teens / by Gail B. Stewart; photographer Carl Franzén.
        p. cm. — (The other America)
    Includes bibliographical references and index.
    Summary: Discusses the numbers of homeless teenagers, their situation
and behavior, and looks at the lives of four of them.
    ISBN 1-56006-398-X (lib. : alk. paper)
    1. Homeless youth—United States—Juvenile literature. [1. Homeless
persons.   2. Homelessness.] I. Title. II. Series.
Stewart, Gail B. 1949–   Other America.
HV4505.S8   1999
362.7'086'942—dc21   98-37997
                                                                           CIP
                                                                            AC

Printed in the U.S.A.
Copyright © 1999 by Lucent Books, Inc.
P.O. Box 289011, San Diego, CA 92198-9011

Contents

Foreword

O, YES,
I SAY IT PLAIN,
AMERICA NEVER WAS AMERICA TO ME.
AND YET I SWEAR THIS OATH—
AMERICA WILL BE!
LANGSTON HUGHES

Perhaps more than any other nation in the world, the United States represents an ideal to many people. The ideal of equality—of opportunity, of legal rights, of protection against discrimination and oppression. To a certain extent, this image has proven accurate. But beneath this ideal lies a less idealistic fact—many segments of our society do not feel included in this vision of America.

They are the outsiders—the homeless, the elderly, people with AIDS, teenage mothers, gang members, prisoners, and countless others. When politicians and the media discuss society's ills, the members of these groups are defined as what's wrong with America; they are the people who need fixing, who need help, or increasingly, who need to take more responsibility. And as these people become society's fix-it problem, they lose all identity as individuals and become part of an anonymous group. In the media and in our minds these groups are identified by condition—a disease, crime, morality, poverty. Their condition becomes their identity, and once this occurs, in the eyes of society, they lose their humanity.

The Other America series reveals the members of these groups as individuals. Through in-depth interviews, each person tells his or her unique story. At times these stories are painful, revealing individuals who are struggling to maintain their integrity, their humanity, their lives, in the face of fear, loss, and economic and spiritual hardship. At other times, their tales are exasperating, demonstrating a litany of poor choices, shortsighted thinking, and self-gratification. Nevertheless, their identities remain distinct, their personalities diverse.

As we listen to the people of *The Other America* series describe their experiences, they cease to be stereotypically defined and become tangible, individual. In the process, we may begin to understand more profoundly and think more critically about society's problems. When politicians debate, for example, whether the homeless problem is due to a poor economy or lack of initiative, it will help to read the words of the homeless. Perhaps then we can see the issue more clearly. The family who finds itself temporarily homeless because it has always been one paycheck from poverty is not the same as the mother of six who has been chronically chemically dependent. These people's circumstances are not all of one kind, and perhaps we, after all, are not so very different from them. Before we can act to solve the problems of the Other America, we must be willing to look down their path, to see their faces. And perhaps in doing so, we may find a piece of ourselves as well.

Introduction

THE FACTS ABOUT HOMELESS TEENS

Patsy is a fifteen-year-old from Gary, Indiana. She and her two sisters lived with their mother in a three-bedroom apartment—until last November. The previous summer her mother lost her job at the printing company where she had worked for three years and, as a result, was unable to make the rent payments. The family was forced to move three months later. Low-income housing was scarce in the city, however, and Patsy's mother decided instead to move to Chicago, where she had relatives.

But Chicago was a disappointment; they stayed with Patsy's aunt and her family for three weeks, but it became clear that there were simply too many people living under one roof. Patsy's family has been in a shelter for two weeks now, hoping that her mother can find work so that they can afford a place of their own.

Buddy is thirteen and is homeless, too. He has been in trouble at school and at home, and although his teachers suspect there is trouble at home, they have no idea how much trouble. Buddy's father and mother use crack and often neglect him and his three younger brothers. Even though he felt he was abandoning his brothers, Buddy left home in January. He's met some other homeless teenagers, and they have shown him tricks to survive on his own, such as dumpster diving for leftover food and panhandling. He sleeps in abandoned buildings or, in nicer weather, under a bridge. His parents have not reported him missing.

A PROBLEM OUT OF CONTROL

Buddy and Patsy are just two of dozens of homeless teens whose stories have helped in the research for this book. Their stories, unfortunately, are not at all uncommon; thousands of teenagers are homeless throughout the United States. Their numbers are growing, too, and they've got experts worried.

"Homelessness among adolescents is up by almost 25 percent in the last five years," says one youth advocacy counselor. "We know many of the reasons that contribute to it, but that doesn't help us work through this problem. We can *know* that more kids are neglected and abused at home, or we can *know* that more families with teenage children are falling through the economic cracks. Okay, we know! But what can be done about it? That's the frustrating part."

Other youth workers agree. "Being homeless for anyone is calamitous," says a housing adviser in Minneapolis. "It puts a huge amount of stress on people who are already struggling with things like poverty or drug abuse. But with kids, the problems seem to intensify. They're asked to deal with a lot of things at such a terribly young age."

WHO ARE THE HOMELESS?

There are many specific reasons why teens are homeless. For about one-third of the homeless teens in the United States, their parents' situation has caused their homelessness.

Thirteen-year-old Alicia is an example. She is staying in a shelter with her family. Her mother is on welfare, and the apartment in which they were living has been condemned. Unable to meet the requirements of a down payment and rent at another apartment building, the family has no other option.

"We don't want to live in some neighborhood where all they're doing is turning tricks and selling crack," says Sofia, Alicia's mother. "But at this point, I'd take anything. I don't want my girls here in this shelter. I'm still working, still going to my job every day, but I don't like them alone here. What can I do?"

The second category of homeless teens is made up of both runaways and "throwaways"—those teens whose parents have made it clear that they are not welcome at home.

Sixteen-year-old Robert is a throwaway. His father has been telling him for over a year that life would be better if Robert weren't around. "I got in trouble a couple of times," says Robert, "and both times I ended up in the police station. I'm a juvenile, so I go to JC [juvenile corrections]. But when the intake worker calls my house, my dad doesn't come to get me.

"I sit in there for five or six days, and they process me out; I go to another facility. One time I even got put in foster care. So I ran away from foster care. Out on the street, maybe they say I'm a runaway—I don't know what my chart says. But ask my dad— he all but pushed me out."

Runaways and throwaways are increasing dramatically, and their average age is dropping. "We see lots and lots of kids younger than twelve or thirteen now," says Chris Rowan, a counselor for a halfway house for teens. "They look like babies to me, just young and vulnerable. Lots of them left or felt pushed out because of sexual abuse or some form of substance abuse. Lots of them are depressed. And when you look in their eyes, every last one of them is scared!"

THE NUMBERS

Getting an accurate idea of how big the homeless teen population is can be extremely tricky. As with the homeless population in general, the numbers depend on who is doing the counting as well as who is being counted.

For example, the U.S. Department of Housing and Urban Development (HUD) tends to have much lower estimates of America's homeless population (about 475,000) than advocacy groups such as the National Coalition for the Homeless and the Partnership for the Homeless (between 2.5 and 4 million). HUD officials complain that the advocacy organizations are inflating their estimates to draw more attention to their cause. On the other hand, the advocacy organizations are critical of HUD, saying that the government organization uses far too narrow a definition of homelessness— only those who live in shelters or on the streets. The homeless who live in cars, vacant buildings, or tents are not counted. Nor is the large segment of homeless who temporarily "couch crash" with friends, neighbors, or family members.

"FREE AND INVISIBLE"

The homeless teen population is even more difficult to count, especially those who are on their own, running from (or having been thrown out by) their families. These young people often tend to avoid agencies and shelters, especially if they feel that they are being sought by juvenile authorities or the police.

One sixteen-year-old who was interviewed for this book attested to the fact that police tend to be regulars at homeless shelters. "Detectives come in a lot, bringing pictures of who they're looking for, or sometimes a warrant," she says. "They go to the front desk where you're registered—you have to give your name and your social security number, see? And they check that. And in case you're using a different name, they just ask everybody, 'Have you seen her?' or whatever. They keep coming by, checking."

Little wonder, say those who work with runaway youth, that homeless teens tend to live more in the shadows, choosing not to seek help from agencies or shelters. "I know lots of kids who've never been in a shelter, and they've been homeless for years," says Ida, a homeless seventeen-year-old from Georgia. "They beg for money or they dumpster dive; they don't go to clinics or anything—anywhere they'd have to give their name or anything, they avoid. So that way they can stay free and invisible."

TEENS AT RISK

No matter which agency does the counting, however, most experts agree that children and teens are the fastest-growing segment of the homeless population—increasing by almost 40 percent between 1993 and 1997. This dramatic increase has youth workers worried. They point to the dangers of the streets, noting that young people are more susceptible to them than most.

"I worry because teenagers are such quick-change artists," says one counselor. "They can seem so very grown up—forming sexual relationships, for example—while inside they can be so very young and naive. So many of the teenage runaways and homeless are very vulnerable, very much at risk of modeling the wrong sorts of behavior—whether it's drug use, criminal activity, or sexual behavior. If they are homeless and on their own, they are without adequate supervision—period."

Even homeless teens who live with their parents are at risk. Antoinette is a homeless mother of twin thirteen-year-old girls. She is busy during the day, making the rounds of social workers, agencies, and employment opportunities, and she can't be there to supervise her daughters.

"I know what sorts of people are in these shelters," she says, aware of the apparent irony. "And I'm not including myself or my girls—we're here just temporarily because of hard times. But you know what class of people are in these shelters? It's crackheads, it's drunks, that's who. It's a lot of lowlifes who are looking for a free bed because they've got no idea of what they're about. I don't want [my daughters] around with those people."

If families are worried about the free time of their teenage children in homeless shelters, the teens themselves are often in agreement.

"I hate it here," says Ray, fifteen. "We've been in this shelter for four weeks. My mom takes me and Tasha [age six] with her when she goes to the government building. Every day we wait for her, and it's really boring. But we can't stay at the shelter because you've got to be out of there by 7:30 every morning, and there's nowhere for us to go. Mom won't let us go to the park by ourselves."

A Lack of Continuity

In addition to the boredom (and dangers) of too much free time, homeless teens face another problem—a lack of continuity. Adolescence is a time when young people need consistency, whether it be in their friendships, in the discipline instilled by their parents, or their education. Homelessness, especially when the teen is on his or her own, can disrupt all of these things, often with disastrous results.

"I feel so badly for many of the young people I see," says a homeless teen counselor in St. Paul. "They have experienced upheavals that can destroy the rest of their lives. They miss six months of school, or maybe a year, or even two. Friendships are put on hold—and friendships are often the one constant thing in the teen's life up till then."

Another runaway advocate agrees. "People talk about the resiliency of youth," he says. "Kids are supposed to be able to bounce back from anything. But I don't buy it, at least most of the time. There are too many important things these kids are missing when they are without a home for any length of time, especially when they are on their own. There are too many ways for them to fall through the cracks."

"Know What You're Getting Into"

The Other America: Homeless Teens tells the stories of four young people. Each is, or has been, homeless for different reasons.

Thirteen-year-old Alvin is a smart eighth grader who is currently residing in a shelter with his parents and younger brother. His parents both suffer from substance abuse problems, and they were in the process of divorcing before circumstances plunged them into homelessness. Alvin wants his parents to stay together, and he hopes that "being in the shelter together will make us a family again."

Nina, sixteen, became a veteran of shelters after her mother's addiction to crack destroyed her home life. She has been in and out of a gang and has wrestled with her own drug use. Nina maintains that this experience has taught her valuable lessons she would never have learned in school.

Andre, seventeen, was a drug dealer in Michigan until his mother made him move out. After living with relatives for a time, Andre got a job at a fast food restaurant, determined to change the way he was living. He now sleeps on a coworker's couch, preferring this arrangement to shelter life. Andre wishes he'd listened more to his mother when he was younger, and he advises teens who are contemplating leaving home to think twice. "Know what you're getting into," he says. "It ain't fun."

Athena is a nineteen-year-old throwaway who has seen "more of the street than I'd ever imagined." After being rejected by both of her parents, Athena began living in shelters, under bridges, in parks, and in abandoned buildings. Today she has battled back from drug addiction, poor health, and homelessness, and is now living in transitional housing for at-risk youth.

Alvin

"I GO TO THE SAME SCHOOL AS
BEFORE. . . . IT WAS KIND OF
WEIRD AT FIRST. . . . I DIDN'T
KNOW FOR SURE HOW MY
FRIENDS WOULD REACT. I DON'T
HIDE IT OR ANYTHING LIKE THAT.
. . . I GUESS IF SOMEONE'S YOUR
FRIEND, THEY'RE NOT GOING TO
THINK YOU'RE WEIRD FOR
SOMETHING LIKE THIS. THAT'S
JUST LIFE, I GUESS. PEOPLE
HAVE UPS AND DOWNS."

Author's Note: Alvin, thirteen, is staying with his parents and his younger brother in a shelter just north of the city. He has been homeless for a few months, but he has only been at the shelter a few weeks. He is a bright, interesting eighth grader, who in many ways seems to be more of an adult than either of his parents—both of whom are dealing with their own problems.

It's seven o'clock at the shelter, and Alvin and his mother are waiting in the lobby. It's noisy there, with the comings and goings of families with small children who are unhappy with the idea of being inside on a warm May evening. People stroll in from various soup kitchens and free dining halls; they show their passes to the desk clerk, who buzzes the door open for them.

"Let's go outside," Alvin suggests. "It's nice outside."

His mother, Anna, a worried-looking woman with a bruised temple and a freshly cast arm in a blue-and-white sling, nods. She wordlessly follows her son outside and sits next to him on a small patch of grass on the east side of the building.

Alvin is a handsome boy, with long, dark hair brushed straight back from his face. His eyes are dark, with long lashes. He is slightly shorter than an average eighth grader, and he has a slim build. Even so, he says with a smile, he's got lots of girlfriends.

"I don't really go looking for them," he says. "I guess they just find me. There's one girl I like, but it's nothing special, not worth mentioning. Besides, there isn't much future in it, making attachments like that. I don't even know where we'll be living by next week."

Alvin's parents have many problems caused by their excessive drinking. His mother, leaning on Alvin, had her arm broken by a man who broke into a house in which she was staying.

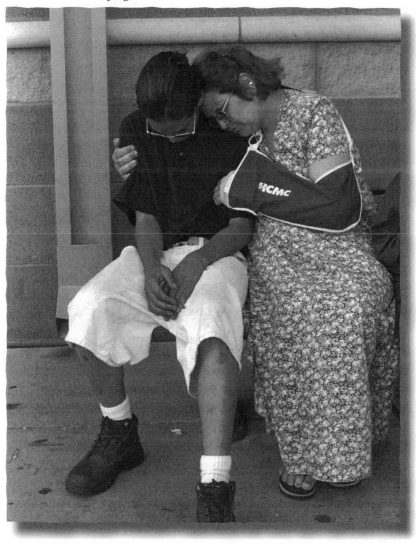

"THERE'VE BEEN LOTS OF COMPLAINTS ABOUT US"

Alvin explains that he and his family have been homeless, on and off, for more than a month. The reasons are complex, although he admits that one of the main reasons is that landlords tend not to like his family.

"I guess you could say," he begins, looking at his mother for permission to speak, "that my family likes to have a good time."

Does this mean drinking? He nods.

"Yeah, they drink. I guess there've been lots of complaints about us, in most of the places we lived," he says. "My parents and their friends have parties, like late at night, and have fun with their friends. They crank the music up pretty loud and go till after two in the morning. And when the neighbors complain, the landlord gets called, and we get in trouble.

"Plus, in the house that we were living at, one guy broke in and caused some damage. It wasn't like a burglar, no; it was one of my parents' friends. Well, he used to be their friend. Anyway, he was real drunk and came in when we were sleeping one night, looking for a place to stay. He busted the door pretty good and threw some stuff around until we got him settled down, and then he went to sleep. And the landlord didn't like that, either."

Anna, sitting stoically as her son speaks, now clears her throat.

"Yeah, the good times are part of the reason I left," she says. "See, I left my husband, Jeff, and my boys. Me and Jeff, we even got divorce papers. The drinking was getting out of hand. I have a real problem with alcohol, and I was getting worse. When I left them I stopped drinking for a while. But then I got lonesome because I was used to having a big family around all the time—and I started drinking again.

"I'm back with my family again, in this shelter, for the time being," she says. "They were homeless before I was. But then I got beat up by this guy who broke into the place I was staying. See this cast? He used a bat, broke my arm in two places, and my wrist, too. So when I got out of the hospital I had nowhere to go, so I came here."

MOVING, AND MOVING AGAIN

Alvin says that when his mother left, he and his father and younger brother were only able to stay in their home a short while before the landlord finally kicked them out.

"He told us he was selling the house and that he had to get us out," he remembers. "But then he had some other lady in there not long afterwards. He lied to us—that's for sure. It was all about the neighbors, just like always.

"But we weren't homeless from that," he says. "We moved into an apartment right next door to the house we'd been in. But the landlord wasn't taking care of that place—the roof was like falling apart. It was really bad, so we ended up moving from there, too. That's when we went and stayed for a little while with my mom, where she was staying. But that didn't last very long. And one day it's like me and my little brother and my dad, we didn't have any-place to live. So we came here to this shelter."

Anna nods and adds that the story behind her homelessness is a bit more frightening than a leaking roof.

"When I left my husband," she says, "I moved in with a boy-friend. Then after a while he kicked me out. Then this guy who was a friend of my boyfriend, he lets me move in with him. I was there for about three months, but things really didn't work out."

"HE'D BEEN USING DRUGS"

Anna says that the man she was living with flunked a urinalysis test, which was mandatory because he was an offender. When asked what he had done, she looks uncomfortable.

"I'd rather not say," she says, nervously picking pieces of grass. Then, reconsidering, she says, "My own mother couldn't under-stand why I was staying there in the first place with a man who would do that. See, he was sexually abusing his own daughter."

She steals a quick look up to gauge my reaction.

"And my own father had been an alcoholic and had done the same to me—that's why my mother was so amazed I'd stay with this guy. Did I know it was happening? Yeah, I knew it was going on—more or less. I guess I thought it was my fault or something. I was mixed up—I still am, I guess.

"Anyway, he flunked his urinalysis test. He'd been using drugs, hiding it from me. He was keeping weed in his dresser drawer, being sneaky like that. And just after that, before I had a chance to figure out what I was going to do, where I was going to go, I got beat up.

"The guy that beat me up was crazy. I had met the guy in a bar—he followed me home and I told him to leave. I said, 'What are you doing coming here—I'm living with a guy!' But he was mad, and he came back another time with a bat. He would have killed me, too—I jumped out a window just in time. And like I told you, when I got out of the hospital I didn't have anywhere to go. So that's how I got homeless."

MEETING UP

Alvin has been listening to his mother, and although he first snickered at the idea of her boyfriends, the topic seems to have made him sad.

"My mom went to a different shelter first," he says. "It's just across the highway, see? But it was really crustified, really a ghetto. It had men on one side, women on the other. But this place, where we are now, is really clean. Plus it's all families—either with both parents or one. So we asked Mary Jo, the lady who runs it, if Mom could move in with us for a while, and she said yes. I'm glad, yeah. We're all together, and that's good. We should be a family, even though we came here separate."

Alvin admits that it is not just his mother who has problems.

"My dad is an alcoholic, I guess you'd have to say," he admits. "I mean, he's not the worst drinker you've ever seen, but it seems like it's a real problem for him. But here at the shelter there's no drinking and no drugs allowed. If you use them, you have to leave. And my dad's been sober ever since we got here.

"I like it better when he's sober, too," he goes on. "Sometimes when he's drunk I forget that he's even there because he's like out of it, you know? But now, I always know he's around. It's better."

THE OTHER LIFE

Besides his parents' drunken parties, what was life like before he was homeless? Alvin pauses, thinking. He takes a plastic bag filled with suckers out of his pocket and slowly unwraps one.

"It was sometimes fun," he says. "Back when we were at that house, we lived not too far from a park. After school I'd go outside, play baseball or football. My cousin Junior would come around— he's okay, but my mom can't stand him."

Anna makes a disgusted noise in the back of her throat.

"No, I can't," she agrees. "He's got a record, done lots of robberies, breaking into cars and whatnot, and is lucky not to be in jail, if you ask me. He's in a gang, too. I don't have much good to say about him."

"But he's my cousin," says Alvin. "I'll always love him, that's the way it is. I know he's made a lot of mistakes, though. He and my older brothers kind of walk the same line. My older brothers are up north now, living with my uncle. They get in trouble if they're down here in the city, so it's best for them to be gone. But anyway, Junior came around and we hung out sometimes.

"I like sports a lot—that's probably my favorite thing to do," he continues. "When I was in grade school, I used to go to this group called Golden Eagles that's for Native American kids. They had a bus and picked you up from school sometimes. You'd play on teams in leagues they had or you'd go places, they'd take you on little trips. I really liked it—it was fun to get out and see things. But the bus doesn't come to the school where I'm at now. I don't do that anymore."

"I DON'T HIDE IT"

Is living in a shelter embarrassing to Alvin? Has he been able to tell his friends about it? He shrugs.

Alvin plays cards with his father. Alvin's father is an alcoholic, but Alvin hopes that by staying at the shelter, where drinking is not allowed, his father may sober up.

"I go to the same school as before," he explains. "And yeah, it was kind of weird at first, I guess. I didn't know for sure how my friends would react. I don't hide it or anything like that. Now some of them know, and some of them don't. The ones who know are okay with it. I guess if someone's your friend, they're not going to think you're weird for something like this. That's just life, I guess. People have ups and downs.

"My teachers don't know. And my principal doesn't know. I don't really have any teachers that I'm close to. I don't have any

Alvin has a hard time telling teachers and friends about being homeless: "I don't really have any teachers that I'm close to. I don't have any relationship with them at all."

relationship with them at all, to tell you the truth. I like gym class, but my gym teacher's mean—he yells at you for little things. I like my reading teacher okay, her name's Miss Stocker. But I don't go talking to teachers like some kids do. That just would feel funny, going to talk to a teacher. I just don't like them, I guess."

Alvin looks sideways at his mother, who has been listening intently.

"In a way, it's harder when your parents split up than when you get homeless," he says, choosing his words carefully. "I didn't even know they were getting divorced, even though they fought sometimes. I just was looking for a pencil one day and just happened across these documents that said 'Divorce' something-or-other. It felt very weird."

He shakes his head, looking down at the grass. "I mean, I thought you didn't stop loving somebody after seventeen years, that's all. I just thought people didn't stop loving. They should forgive, that's what they should do."

He stops talking. Anna continues to look down. For a few minutes, we all sit in silence.

LIFE AT THE SHELTER

After a while, Anna says quietly, "Tell about what Mary Jo does on Mondays." She continues to look down at the ground when she talks to her son. "Tell what happens then."

"Oh, yeah," says Alvin. "She comes around to all the kids and gives everybody a dollar. It's sort of like allowance, I guess. Even the little kids get it. That way you can get pop out of the machine or use the money for whatever you want. She does that twice a week—except on Thursdays she gives you two dollars. Just for spending money.

"I don't have much money usually. That's one thing that's hard. But Mary Jo's pretty nice. If you ask her, she'll let you volunteer to do a job, like wipe down tables, or sweeping, or clean up outside. She'll pay you a little bit to do jobs. She wants kids to be busy, not just hanging around.

"The deal here is you have to obey the rules," says Alvin seriously. "I think the rules are pretty fair, actually. You have to behave, and no fighting. You've got to treat people with respect, even little kids. No mouthing off to people who work here, even if they are being unfair. And you're supposed to be grateful and appreciative. You can make noise and run around outside on the playground, but not inside. It's like a dormitory or a hotel or something."

Alvin says that this shelter is far better than others in the city, and people are usually more than willing to obey the rules here.

"It's nice here because there's room. In a way it's nicer than where we used to live! I don't like being homeless, but if you have to be homeless, this is a good place to stay until you can get back on your feet. There's a little recreation room, besides the outside part with the swings and basketball hoop. And they've got a whole bunch of balls they'll let you use for free."

FRIENDS DON'T COME AROUND

Alvin has not seen many of his friends since his family arrived at the shelter, although he says that he *could* invite them over to play outside.

"They aren't allowed upstairs though," he says. "They only let the people who are supposed to be here up, just the families. I guess they don't want outsiders bringing in drugs or stuff to the people. Outsiders don't have anything at stake—they don't care whether Mary Jo kicks them out or not. But the people here don't want to get kicked out.

"You get a certain amount of time here—maybe a month at the most. You're supposed to use that time getting your life together. The grown-ups are supposed to find a job, line up a place to live. If you don't do that, you're out. And like I said, if you don't obey the rules, you're out, too."

Alvin admits he misses seeing Junior and a few of his other friends from his old neighborhood.

"Junior hasn't ever been here," he says, glancing over at his mother. "And I know my mom is glad. The last time she saw him, he was in pretty bad shape."

"He was cracked out, that's what," Anna grumbles. "He was using our phone, yelling at his girlfriend. He was abusing her, the way he talked. I didn't like that at all."

"Yeah," remembers Alvin, "he got really mad at my mom because she told him he couldn't use the phone if he talked like that to his girlfriend. He was yelling at her—really got mad.

"Anyway, Junior wouldn't like it around here even if he was allowed to stay. They've got a curfew of 8:30—even on weekends. That's way earlier than the curfew the county has for someone my age! But it's easier to get up earlier in the morning if you go to bed earlier. My school bus comes here to the shelter, picks me up outside. Then when I come home, there's kids around here to play with. We just play around, invent games or whatever. It's fine."

GETTING HIS FATHER BACK ON TRACK

Before they were kicked out of their home, Alvin says, his father had a good job in a hospital.

Alvin likes the predictability and pleasantness of the shelter, which is an improvement over the chaotic life he led with his parents. "There's a little recreation room, . . . and basketball hoop. And they've got a whole bunch of balls they'll let you use for free."

"He was a triage technician," he says proudly. "That's the guy in the emergency room who looks at all the people coming in and figures out who needs medical attention first. There's lots of emergencies he sees—gunshot wounds, stabbings, car accidents, whatever. And he gets to make the decision who the doctors need to look at right away. It's real important."

Anna nods. "It's a real skilled position. He had to go to two years of college downtown here to learn to do it. I went to college for a while, too. We didn't meet there—we met in a bar."

She giggles, and Alvin smiles. "Yeah, she bought him a drink because he was so good-looking!" he says, laughing.

"Anyway," Anna says, "the job was good; it paid—what?—twenty-one dollars an hour, I think. But he isn't working there anymore. He's not doing much of anything right now."

Alvin stops smiling and looks uncomfortable. "He told me that he doesn't want to work anymore until he sobers up for good," he says defensively. "See, after she left us, my dad didn't want to leave us boys alone—he was working night shifts then. So he had to quit his job so he could take care of us. So we got on welfare, and then we moved, and—well, you know the rest. So he figures he can't work again since his drinking has been pretty bad. He's okay right now, right at this minute, but he wants to get everything under control."

What does his father do every day at the shelter? Alvin thinks.

"He sometimes works temporary stuff," he says vaguely. "And he plays a lot of cards. He plays this one game of solitaire—he really gets into it."

PLANS TO MOVE

Buddy wanders outside, looking for his brother. He is a stocky boy of nine, with a quick smile. He waves shyly and sits next to his brother.

"Me and Buddy and my dad have been talking a lot lately about what we're going to do when we leave here," he says. "I think one thing that's likely to happen is going up to Duluth, way up north. We'd stay with my great-auntie. She had a stroke or something, and she wants my father to come up there and take care of her. She thinks he could also get a job in a hospital there part-time, too, so that would be good."

"Duluth is in Minnesota," Buddy offers helpfully. "It's right next to a lake."

Alvin and his brother Buddy play in the shelter's recreation yard. The boys look forward to their future as their dad promises them a more stable life. "I feel better having a plan like that," Alvin remarks.

"I feel better having a plan like that," says Alvin. "It makes the other stuff seem less important, like the stuff at school, like missing out on the field trip to Valleyfair."

His mother frowns. "What about the field trip?"

Alvin says, "I can't go because I lost the fourteen dollars. Even if I had the money now, it's too late. My teacher said so."

Anna shakes her head. "I didn't know about that."

"But that's okay," he says. "Like I said, going to Duluth will be more fun than going on rides and stuff. Anyway, I've already been to Valleyfair a couple years ago. And lots of other kids aren't going. Besides, maybe I'll go with Andrew and his auntie later this summer. Andrew is my best friend," he explains. "I haven't seen him in a very long time because he goes to some boarding school out in South Dakota or something. He was getting beat up at his school here in the city, that's why he doesn't go to school here anymore. But we'll get together, and I bet his Auntie Nancy will take us. She's nice."

"She is," Buddy agrees. "She once gave me a Bulls T-shirt."

A MOTHER'S POINT OF VIEW

The conversation stops quickly as the ice cream truck rings its bell. On nice days the truck comes to the shelter, and there is always a line.

"Can we?" Buddy asks his mother. She pulls out a dollar from her pocket and tells them she wants change. Alvin and Buddy jump up quickly and run over to the line.

"I feel bad for the way things are turning out," she says softly. "I learned early about not having much respect for myself. I guess it was my own dad that taught me. When we were small he'd beat my mom up all the time. She'd go out looking for him, and I'd go with her. We'd take the car. And lots of times, you'd see him with women. That was bad."

She sighs, readjusting her legs. "I'm just getting tired of feeling bad all the time. It isn't good for my boys to see me like this. I just turned forty, but sometimes I feel like I'm eighty. It's real hard for me to think about leaving this place, too. I worry about when I leave, how we'll probably see our old friends again, and then we might start drinking, you know? You get back in the same old habits with your friends. But then I think, what if I let them go to Duluth without me and I get lonesome? I'll feel so bad, so guilty that I'm not there for my boys.

"I don't want to be separated from my boys anymore. I love them, all four of them. The two older ones are doing okay up north, but Buddy is too young to be away from me. And Alvin— he's a real good boy, but he needs his mother, too."

She starts to cry. "Those parties were a problem. We'd go to the liquor store—'case up,' we called it. We'd get three or four cases of beer and sit around all night. That's no life for the boys, and sometimes I feel real ashamed that those are the memories they'll always have. I've got to get myself straightened out, I think. I'm not much good to anybody now. And Mary Jo's helping me get into a program for battered women, so I stop getting involved with people who abuse me. Jeff, my ex, he never did that. But we just argue too much, that's our problem. I don't see any way out from that."

"I'M *TOO GOOD* FOR IT"

Alvin and Buddy return with cherry Popsicles and hand Anna two quarters.

"Thanks, Mom," Buddy says, peeling the paper off.

Anna smiles. "I like to see them happy. It seems like there haven't been enough happy times lately. Plus, I worry about these guys growing up. It just seems like there are so many wrong turns a kid can take these days—look at my older two! They got into the gangs, into the crime, into the stuff going on out on the street corners."

Alvin shakes his head. "I'm not going to be like that. You know why? 'Cause I'm *too good* for it. I know that some people like to do that, and it's sometimes hard to avoid it, but not for me. That's them. That's their fault."

But what about Junior? Doesn't his closeness with his cousin make gang life more tempting?

"No," he says. "I'm not *that* close to Junior, where I'm going to be his little crime buddy. I don't need to do things like that to feel good. I know what's going on, and I have my own thoughts. I'm not just going to follow him, my brothers, or anyone else.

"I look at my brothers. They've been in jail for stupid things. My brother Danny was a Gangster Disciple, just like my brother Marty was. But they weren't trying to get me in—they were being overprotective. They wanted me to stay out of trouble."

"I DON'T WANT TO GET IN REAL TROUBLE"

Alvin says that even though some people blame their situations on bad luck, he thinks many times people get into situations that tempt bad results.

"Like my brother Danny," he says. "He got caught robbing a house and didn't show up for his court date. They never came for him; it seemed like maybe he was going to get away without going to trial. But then one day he's crossing the street and he gets hit by a taxicab. And at the hospital, Danny got caught—some cops came and arrested him because he had that warrant out. That was the day he was getting released from the hospital.

"Somebody might say that was bad luck, but Danny shouldn't have been robbing houses in the first place. He got in a position where he was going to get in trouble, either sooner or later. So they

In spite of his rough life, Alvin's attitude sets him apart. He insists he will not get involved in the illegal activities many other young people his age get involved in. "I'm too good for it. I know that some people like to do that . . . but not for me," he vows.

took him to juvenile hall, then to a youth ranch up north. Now he's on probation, living with my uncle. When Danny comes down here to visit, he gets in trouble again. That's so stupid."

Alvin looks disgusted. "I wish my brothers weren't like that, but they are. But I'm not. I've been in some trouble before—not bad trouble, but trouble. And I learned that I don't want to get in real trouble like my brothers did."

A LITTLE TROUBLE

Alvin says that he was in juvenile hall himself once, and he intends never to go back.

"It was for something really stupid," he says. "I got caught by police setting off fireworks. I was in my backyard, in that house we got kicked out of, you know? And those neighbors called the cops—told them I was playing around with a gun. So the cops came, and they kept asking me, 'Where's the gun? Where's the gun?' I kept telling them, 'No, it's fireworks.'

"They believed me. I mean, they had to, because they could see the little bag I had with firecrackers in it. And I had matches, and they could see the stuff, the papers from the fireworks on the ground. But they said they had to be sure because the neighbors had been real sure that I had a gun. So they searched my house, looking for a gun. There wasn't a gun, just like I said.

"But I had to stay the night in jail and wait for a court appearance the next morning. It was just fireworks, but that's illegal, so I got warned. It was last summer, when I was twelve. It was really stupid."

Alvin says there were a few other encounters with the police, but they too were minor.

"I got picked up sometimes for being out after curfew," he says. "Stuff like that. It was never anything bad—I wouldn't do anything bad. A couple of fights, though. Just fistfights with some Mexican kids that started something at the store. They were drunk, and I was walking by with my friend Kevin. We said 'hi' to the one guy, and he took out a knife!

"Well, we picked up rocks and started throwing them. My dad and his friends were around, too, and they kind of got into it. It never amounted to anything, but like I said, it taught me that I didn't want to get in the justice system. It's not worth it."

When asked whether he's looking forward to anything in the near future, Alvin frowns.

"I don't know," he says, slowly unpeeling another sucker from his plastic bag. "I sort of look forward to getting out of here, but sort of not, you know? Because if we don't go to Duluth, if something happens and our plans change—then it might be bad. I don't want to count on anything good happening because then you get disappointed.

"I guess I *can* count on my best friend, Andrew. It's funny how we don't see each other that much, but we can be best friends again the minute we do. I met him one time when I was at my friend Johnny's apartment. We were looking for an adapter for the Sega game, and I just knocked on his door. We got to talking, and he was really nice. So we just started doing things together.

"So anyway, he got back last Sunday, and he called me up right away. We'll do some stuff—and like I told you before, his Auntie Nancy will do things with us. She's so nice—she's like a friend to us. I look forward to that stuff happening."

Alvin says that it's easier to think of good things happening in the far-off future than in the next weeks or months.

"I think about what I'd like to do when I grow up," he says. "I know one thing that sounds cool—being one of those medevac nurses. They are the ones who fly around in helicopters, airlifting people and saving their lives. A guy came to my school once—he was one of those medevac nurses. He talked to us about it, and I was real impressed.

"I told my dad about that, and he said no way could he do that—he's afraid of heights. He'd be up there and faint."

Alvin shares a chuckle with his brother and mother. "Yeah, he'd be the guy in the little bed, strapped to the side of the helicopter, and *I'd* be taking care of *him!*

"Anyway, that's fun to think about. I can't think of anything else I'd like to be."

Buddy interrupts. "You could be an artist—you're really good at drawing."

Alvin makes a face. "I can just copy stuff, like cartoons. I can't come up with the ideas on my own. I don't think I could make any money copying things. I think that helicopter deal is much smarter for me."

"It's Easier for Me"

Alvin says that he doesn't want to give anybody the impression that being homeless is no big deal. Even though they are in a nice shelter, there are drawbacks.

"Maybe it's easier for me—I'm a teenager, so maybe I can adjust better than Buddy can," he says. "He gets grumpy a lot. He likes running around and having fun. That's what he enjoys. He's still a youngster—he doesn't understand what's going on between my

Alvin sits talking with his best friend Andrew. Alvin depends on his friends, particularly Andrew, to talk to about his life.

mom and dad. Plus, he doesn't understand about the drinking, how my dad's working so hard at being sober. Things just aren't like they were."

Buddy keeps his eye on Alvin, listening intently.

"You don't have privacy anymore—being homeless. The room is clean and nice, but it's not *your* room. The workers are pretty nice, but all of a sudden you don't make your own decisions about things. Even your parents don't make the decisions for you. It's the

Alvin and his brother watch television. Both of them miss life outside the shelter: "Buddy misses our television, and lots of other things we don't even know where they are."

shelter, the shelter's rules. You've got to go to bed at a certain time, you've got to get up at a certain time. It's weird for someone to be taking care of you and your parents, giving orders.

"And not having your stuff around is hard. Buddy misses our television, and lots of other things we don't even know where they are. That one landlord—the one who threw us out—he locked our stuff up. He just kept it; I think he gave it to some lady who moved in there. We had clothes, games—just stuff, you know? I wish I had my clothes. And Buddy had a Bulls T-shirt he really liked, but we don't know where it is now.

"It made me mad; for a while after we got thrown out, I'd go by the house, just to check on what was happening there. I'd get the mail and stuff. I wish now I'd tried to get in and grab some of our things. For a while it was there. And then one day I went over there, and there wasn't anything to grab."

XENA

Alvin picks some grass absentmindedly. He looks at his younger brother.

"Buddy misses home, I know," he says. "And I really know how he feels. We used to have this one cat, Xena. As in *Xena, Warrior Princess*, you know? She was at the one house we had, and she went outside a lot. I worried about her when we had to leave. I hoped I'd see her again, but I never did."

"They've got cats in Duluth, though," Buddy announces. "Maybe we'll get a cat of our own when we go there to live."

Alvin shrugs. "Maybe. And maybe we'll get more of your little cars, your Hot Wheels, that got lost."

"BUDDY GETS SAD REAL EASY"

He sighs. "In some ways, this is harder on Buddy, but in other ways it's harder on me. Like, for instance, Buddy gets sad real easy—he feels embarrassed about being homeless, and he doesn't tell any of his friends at school. He's more shy about things like that. That's the sad part for Buddy.

"But it's also easier to get Buddy in a good mood. Like sometimes Mary Jo gives my dad a little money, and we go out to eat. He likes going to McDonald's and getting a Happy Meal. Cheeseburgers. And that gets Buddy happy again. Or on Mondays and Thursdays, they give out bus tokens to all the residents here, and

Alvin struggles to keep up hope for the future while dealing with the inconsistency of his parents. He fantasizes that the shelter is an island where "none of the people from the outside can get in."

we can go out, just get out of here, over to the city."

Buddy smiles. "One nice thing that happened to me is that someone gave me a Beanie Baby dog. It's—what do you call those spotted dogs? Dalmatian?—it's a dalmatian. His name on the tag is Spot, but I named him Spike. It's a tougher name, I think. Some of the girls said that you aren't allowed to rename Beanie Babies, but I think you can. So I did."

Alvin looks up and smiles. "See what I mean?"

ON THE ISLAND

Anna has gotten to her feet. She seems impatient to get upstairs.

"Mom, did I tell you that graduation is next week?" Alvin says quickly. "It's at night. They'll send a school bus for the parents who want to go who don't have cars. So are you going to do that?"

Anna looks surprised. "I didn't know nothing about that. How come we didn't know nothing about that? I don't know if I can go."

Alvin is silent and looks away. Anna stands for a moment, then walks toward the shelter door. Buddy follows her and looks back nervously to see if Alvin is following.

"Sometimes this place seems like an island," Alvin says. "You can see the tall buildings of the city over there. And then there's the freeway bridge. And over there is a busy street we can't cross. Sometimes it's kind of cool to pretend we're stranded here and none of us can get off. And none of the people from the outside can get on. I guess I wouldn't mind that too much."

Nina

"I WAS SO IMMATURE. I SAW THESE
KINGS. . . . I WANTED TO BE LIKE
THEM. THEY WERE NICE TO ME,
AND I JUST THOUGHT THE BEST
THING THAT COULD HAPPEN TO ME
WAS IF I COULD START HANGING
AROUND THEM. . . . I CAME TO
SCHOOL ON THE FIRST DAY IN THIS
NICE DRESS AND SANDALS. AND
BY THE SECOND WEEK, I WAS
WEARING ALL GANG STUFF."

*Author's Note: Sixteen-year-old Nina is an example of a teen whose home-
lessness was a long time coming. Nina's involvement with gangs in high
school, combined with her mother's crack addiction, plummeted them from
a comfortable lifestyle—in which Nina was an honors student—to living
in shelters. Her mother has recently sworn off drugs, but it will be a while
until the two of them have enough money saved to rent a decent apartment.*

The line has formed early; the free dining room for the city's
homeless doesn't open for another hour, but already the sidewalk
outside is crowded. Some are young mothers with toddlers clus-
tered around their legs. There are old people, too, their faces tired
and worn. A few are mentally ill or are on drugs, and they talk to
themselves in loud voices or mutter foul oaths to others standing
nearby.

Near the back of the line is sixteen-year-old Nina. She has
agreed to talk with me, but only if her friends can talk, too.

"We kind of support each other," she explains, smiling. "We
look out for each other—you have to do this if you're homeless

and on the street." She is standing with two older girls—Jennifer, eighteen, and Tanya, nineteen. The three talk in quiet voices. Nina smiles and nods as a younger teen walks by.

"Hey, Margaret," say Nina and Jennifer in unison. Then, turning to me, Nina says, "That's Margaret. She's in the same shelter as us. There's a bunch of us that stay over there, at Harbor Lights shelter. This is where we usually come for breakfast."

Nina eats a meal at the city's free dining room for the homeless. Nina's friends are extremely important to her: "We kind of support each other. We look out for each other."

Getting Breakfast

Is it unusual for so many teenagers to be homeless, on their own in the city? Nina and her friends look at each other a moment, then start to laugh.

"There's so many homeless kids, you can't even imagine," Nina says. "I bet the three of us here could list off at least—what?—probably seventy-five or eighty we know by name."

Her companions consider this and nod emphatically.

"And that's just the ones from around here that we see eating in this place every day," says Jennifer. "There's hundreds more than that, I bet."

We chat for a while until the doors to the dining area open. There is a sense of urgency among the people as the line begins to move. A uniformed police officer stands by the inner door, chewing gum and staring straight ahead.

"They serve a good breakfast here," remarks Nina, peering in the glass window. "There's a lot of variety, you know? Some places, it's not so good. But here you can get pancakes, eggs, beans and rice—lots of stuff. I heard one of the workers say they try to pack on the protein for us."

Inside, workers move quickly, laying out plates of eggs and toast on long tables. As the homeless proceed through the line, they are served by students from a local high school. They are here, says Nina, to get credit for school.

"I see them here a lot," she says. "I think they're in some class where they have to do work helping other people. This is a good place to help; lots of people are needy here. Some of them seem kind of out of place, though, you know? They just act like they'd rather be someplace else."

"I don't blame them," says Jennifer, placing a bowl of hot cereal on her tray. "I wouldn't spend time around this place unless I had to, would you?"

"Right Now, This Is Our Situation"

Nina places her full tray on a table, then announces that she's going to run downstairs to see her mother.

"Her name is Shirley," she says. "And she works here. Today she's sorting clothes people have donated. You can go downstairs and look through the bins—they've got shoes, T-shirts, jeans—just about anything you need. And there's a food shelf down there, too."

38

Nina instructs Tanya and Jennifer to save her place at the table and heads downstairs. She spots her mother right away. Shirley is an attractive, dark-haired woman, although her right eye seems disfigured—the lid not opening completely. She smiles and hugs Nina and spends a few minutes chatting before she announces she has to get back to work.

"She's great," says Nina. "I check in with her a couple times a day. Her eye? That's from two times that my dad beat her. One time he hit her with a four-by-four board. And another time he kicked her in the eye with a steel-toed boot. I was there when it happened.

"Anyway, that's kind of why she and I have been on our own for a long time. See, my mom is homeless, too. I stay in one shelter, and she stays in another place. She's got this job here, and we're hoping to get a place of our own. But right now, this is our situation."

She smiles, leading the way back to the dining room. "And how we got to this point is a long story."

STARTING IN CANADA

Nina spent her early years in Fort Frances, Ontario, where she and her parents lived on a reservation.

"My mom is French Canadian, my father is Native American," she explains. "He lives up there still, but I haven't seen him for a while. He's an alcoholic—he's got a really bad problem with drinking. He always thought she was cheating on him, but she wasn't. But he always blamed her. The first time, when he hit her in the eye with the board, she had surgery. I think it could have healed if he hadn't kicked her with that boot.

"I remember living up there really well," she says. "I used to run out the backdoor, run across the street to my grandma's house. I was always scared when he drank. He didn't *always* drink—but when he did, he was mean. My mom always looked out for me; she'd almost always tell me when to get out of the house."

Did the police arrest him for battering his wife? Nina shakes her head.

"See, on the reservation, we didn't have any direct access to the police. You couldn't just dial 911 like here. The tribal council was in charge; they'd handle problems among the people. And my dad was one of the elders—he was the treasurer of the tribal council! That was his job; my mom didn't have a job in those days. She stayed home, took care of the house. She did take part-time classes at a technical school, learning how to be a welder. But she didn't get a job until after we left."

"THAT'S REAL COMMON"

Jennifer and Tanya have been listening to the story of Nina's mother's beatings and join the conversation.

"That's real common," says Jennifer, an Irish-looking redhead with a freckled face. "You see that a lot among homeless teenagers—abuse, I mean. Now for me, it was my husband. I married real young—I'm eighteen now—and my husband pulled a gun on me and my two-year-old daughter. He also stabbed me twice. Put me in the hospital, he did. That's the whole reason I'm homeless—I'm running away. I've stashed our daughter somewhere safe, and I'm hiding out; I feel like he'd kill me if he found me."

Tanya, a tired-looking blond with black circles under her eyes, agrees.

"I had lots of abuse, too. I was taken away from my biological mom when I was two and sent around to foster families. My mom was a heroin addict and an alcoholic, too."

There are sympathetic murmurs from Nina and Jennifer.

"Anyway, they took me and my brother and sister away. I used to get beat and raped in foster care. I was adopted when I was ten, and my adopted brother was raping me between the ages of ten and thirteen."

"Yuck," says Nina. "Your adopted brother? Did you tell?"

"Yeah, for whatever good it did," Tanya answers in a tired voice. "His parents accused me of teasing him. Yeah, I was a tease—at age ten."

The conversation stops, each girl momentarily silenced by Tanya's story.

MOVING AROUND

Nina speaks first. She assures the others that her father—although terribly troubled by alcoholism—did not abuse *her*.

"I was only little, like two or three," she says. "I could tell by the sound of him coming home in his truck if he was drunk. That's weird, huh? It's like the truck had its own sound, or something. I guess it's that he was driving fast. So I'd hide out, or I'd run away, like I said.

"Anyway, my mom left him after the beatings, and after about two weeks of their separation, she graduated from technical school. She became a welder, and she was real good, too. She's been as high as fifty-three floors, I think. Little tiny bars she can balance on, too—man, I'd never be able to do that. She can do all that, but she says she's still afraid of getting on an airplane!"

Nina picks up a piece of toast and spreads it liberally with strawberry preserves.

Nina and her mother became homeless after her mother became addicted to drugs. Nina witnessed her mother being beaten first by her father then by boyfriends.

"So we moved," she says. "First to International Falls. Then she got a job in Georgia. I guess we were moving to wherever the welding jobs were. But after a while she got bad knees, and she had to learn a new trade. So she became a certified phlebotomist—that's one of those people who draw blood for you at the blood bank. She went to a medical college to learn that. And we came here because she got a job doing that."

CHANGES

Nina says that, for the most part, it was she and her mother—just the two of them.

"We had a nice apartment; her job was great," she says. "We lived south of the city and things seemed great. Then she started going with this guy Nick—they were engaged, in fact. And we moved from our nice apartment to a bigger place. They needed a place that was more roomy because it would be the three of us. The trouble was that it was in a bad area—lots of gangs and drugs and stuff.

"Anyway, about two weeks before they were supposed to get married, Nick went on a rampage! He decided he was going to beat her up. And the next day he went off to work like nothing happened. Well, my mom had had it. No way was she going to get married to him. We packed up all our clothes, all our stuff, and we moved. When he came home, there wasn't a trace of us."

Nina says this proudly, and her friends smile.

"We moved again, just her and I. I guess things were okay for a while, but then I started high school. That's when things fell apart for me. I got permanently kicked out of the public school system in this city, in fact. It's so weird—I'd been a great student in elementary school. I even won this Kiwanis award for scholarship in eighth grade. They give it to one student each school year—just one—for achievement. I had a math level of an eleventh grader—that's one of the reasons I won the award. It's in a gold-plated frame with my name engraved on it."

Nina smiles broadly. "It's really so neat. I'm pretty sure it's in storage somewhere. I hope we didn't lose it. But anyway, I'd been this great student in eighth grade, and then by the second or third week of high school, I was in trouble all the time."

Nina says her trouble began because of gangs at her high school.

"I was so immature," she says. "I saw these Kings—you know,

42

Nina claims that she really doesn't know why she stopped being a good student and became involved in gangs and drugs, but her mother's chaotic behavior probably contributed to her lack of interest.

the Latin Kings? Anyway, I thought they were so cool. I wanted to be like them. They were nice to me, and I just thought the best thing that could happen to me was if I could start hanging around them. I started wearing black and gold, the bandanna, the whole bit. I mean, I came to school on the first day in this nice dress and sandals. And by the second week, I was wearing all gang stuff.

"I started being really bad in school, too. I was doing things I'd never dreamed of. I just wanted to be popular. I'd skip school, I'd go to parties, smoke pot. And the badder I was, the better the Kings liked me."

What kinds of things does one have to do to be permanently barred from the city's schools? Nina winces.

"Well, it started out that I just skipped school a lot," she says. "And nothing was happening to me. The school never called my house—I was getting away with it everyday. They never sent any paper home, nothing. I was loving it!

"Then one day I got in a fight at school. I was getting in a bunch of those—it was real common. But this time I slammed this girl's fingers in a locker—broke four of them. They kicked me out, and my principal drove me home. My mom was there, and he told her about everything. They talked, though, and he allowed me to come back the next week.

"But I screwed up. I whipped a book at a teacher's head, and that's what got me expelled." She grimaces. "Period."

FALLING APART

How could her mother have missed all these signs? How could she have allowed Nina to dress like a gang member, change her circle of friends, and stop trying in school? Nina seems uncomfortable talking about this, but she finally explains that her mother had become addicted to crack, and her addiction made her less involved as a mother.

"After Nick beat her, you know, and we moved, well, she got herself another boyfriend," says Nina. "And he was bad. He was a heroin addict, but he used crack, too. It started for her with a little bit of crack mixed in with some pot. Then she was hooked! After that, she was smoking crack straight.

"I can't really say when she started using it; but it seemed like for a while she was always paying me to get out of the house. See, she didn't want me around to see her. She had *some* pride—I know it seems terrible that she did that, but I give her credit for trying to keep me out of it, you know? She'd give me like sixty or eighty dollars just to get out of the apartment. I remember buying new shoes, new outfits, just spending money."

The money was there then, Nina says, because her mother was still working at the blood bank.

"I wasn't sure why she was being so generous, but I liked it," she says. "One time, when I ran out of money, I went into her room—thinking she was taking a nap or something. But she was in there with her boyfriend, and they were getting high, smoking crack. That was the first time I knew."

What did Nina do after seeing her mother that way?

Nina's mother tells Nina that she has found a job that might allow them to leave the shelter and find a place of their own. It is hard for Nina to depend on her mother after all they have been through.

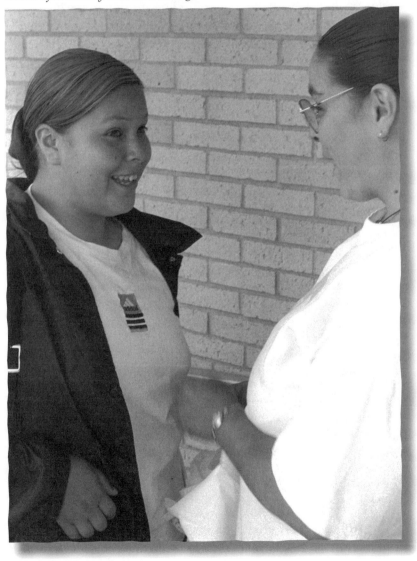

"At first I just stood there looking," says Nina. "I didn't know what to say. But then afterwards we had a talk. I told her how mad it made me, and how scared. She told me she'd stop, and she did—for a while. But crack is really powerful—it's more dangerous than most drugs."

"IT RUINS EVERYTHING"

Tanya nods sympathetically as Nina speaks.

"It's really true," she says. "Crack is so bad—it ruins everything. I bet so many people are homeless because of it, no lie. There's a whole bunch of users that hang around here, getting free meals. You can tell them a mile away—their eyes are dilated, really open wide. They act weird, too."

"Yeah, they are always looking down on the ground," adds Jennifer. "They act all paranoid that people are watching them or something. My ex-husband—the one who beat me—he used crack for three years, so it's easy for me to recognize the signs. It's so addictive; you always want more. Some people can use up a thousand dollars in a day, just buying crack."

Tanya nods. "And it's expensive around here, too. So lots more people are doing crimes just to pay for it. A dime bag here is about half the size of a bag back in Illinois, I know that."

Nina sighs. "I really hate the smell of it, too. It's like old rubber tires burning, I think. Or something real metallic—I don't know. All I know is that when my mom and I had the talk, she had Terrence—that's her addict boyfriend's name—move out. Things seemed like they might get better for a while. But she relapsed. It happened because something really sad happened."

DENNIS

Nina says that the sad thing was the death of Dennis, a boy she had been going out with.

"My mother loved him like a son," she says. "She was so close to him. We let him stay at our house because he was homeless back then, he had no family to love him. They were all back in Honduras, I think. But my mom fed him, put clothes on his back, loved him with all her heart. And then he got killed."

Nina's eyes fill with tears, and she digs in her pocket for a tissue.

"I met Dennis through my gang friends, but he wasn't in a gang. But one of the gangs killed him, for something really stupid.

*Nina sits in a park with her friends. The death of Nina's boyfriend led her
mother to become more heavily involved in drugs. Their situation deteriorated
until they found themselves homeless.*

It was over a girl that he didn't even know. It was mistaken identity, you could say. Someone in the gang thought he was messing
with this girl.

"It wasn't the Kings that killed Dennis, no. It was some gang
from California. They chased him down and shot him. I was on my
way to meet him at the park. I got off the bus and I saw a whole
bunch of police cars. I just had a weird feeling, you know? Like

he'd be dead or something bad had happened to him, anyway. So there he was, lying there with the whole bottom half of his face blown off."

She suddenly looks angry. "It was awful, too; he was shot at 2:45 in the afternoon, but they didn't cover him up for two whole hours. He was just lying there, his feet crossed in back, his head turned. It seemed so disrespectful for the cops to treat him like that. But what do you expect? He was poor, right?"

Jennifer and Tanya nod, agreeing.

THE BEGINNING OF HOMELESSNESS

When Dennis was killed, Nina says, her mother seemed to give up. She lost interest in everything; worst of all, she started smoking crack again.

"She wasn't with a boyfriend or anything," Nina says. "She was just alone; she'd go out and find a dealer and buy what she needed. It was so stupid, too, because she'd had a good job, we had a pretty nice apartment. But things just fell apart.

"For one thing, she wasn't going to work as much. She was more interested in using drugs. And she spent all the money she'd put in savings—man, she smoked that money all up. And then it got worse because my mom started having lots of drug dealers around. These crack dealers are vultures, you know? They just moved in because they knew my mom would let them do anything as long as they gave her drugs.

"She didn't have much money. But they took over the house; used it for selling their drugs. The phone was ringing all the time; it was like they kidnapped our house. They paid her off—either with money or drugs."

Nina remembers that she stopped going back to the apartment, choosing instead to stay with friends.

"I DIDN'T THINK OF IT AS HOMELESS THEN"

"I didn't belong at home anymore," she says. "Everything had changed. I was still acting bad, too—it wasn't just my mom that was being stupid. I was hanging around bad kids. We were robbing people, breaking into cars, breaking windows, popping tires, doing graffiti—just about everything you could name. Plus, I was doing a lot of drinking, smoking pot. I was out of my mind—that's how I explain it now."

Nina hopped from friend to friend, sleeping a few nights with whoever had a spare bed or couch.

"I didn't think of it as homeless then," she says. "It was kind of temporary, I figured. I mean, 'homeless' meant people like that guy over there," she explains, pointing to an old man in a long overcoat singing to himself. "I wasn't like that. I looked at it this way—I was just staying with friends until things in my mom's life settled down."

Jennifer speaks up. "You know, it's real hard to get settled down when you're doing crack. I smoked pot and did a lot of speed, myself. But I never wanted to do crack."

"I didn't either," says Nina. "I tried cocaine one time, but that was unintentional—it was rolled up in a joint, and I smoked it by accident. That was a low point of my life. And I know that crack is real bad—but to me, that addiction is all in your mind. When you get addicted to something it's because you want to be."

Tanya shakes her head emphatically. "No, that's not true," she argues. "There's lots of addictions that aren't in your mind. Heroin, what my mom was on—it's physically addictive, not just in your mind. You can get off it maybe, if you really, really try. But

The entrance to the Salvation Army's Harbor Lights shelter includes a metal detector to prevent residents from bringing weapons into the facility.

it's a bitch. And you can die. My mom was down to eighty-nine pounds and lost all her teeth from heroin. You don't want to mess with it, no kidding. I got off crack myself—but only after I got pneumonia and had a miscarriage. The doctors had to help me. So don't say it's just in your mind."

A FAMILIAR FACE

Nina isn't convinced, but she doesn't want to fight with Tanya. She changes the subject, telling instead how she began staying in the homeless shelter and saw a very familiar face.

"I started running out of places to stay after a while," she says. "I was staying with everyone I could think of—even as far away as Wisconsin. But after a while I was out of luck. No more choices.

"I went to a shelter called Harbor Lights; it's run by the Salvation Army. It's real close to the bus station, so lots of girls go there right after they come to the city. Anyway, I knew right where it was, so I went there.

"So then one day, I see my mother there—right at the shelter! She was staying there, too," says Nina. "She'd gotten thrown out of her apartment, she'd lost her job, everything had fallen apart. And I had sort of hit bottom, too. But I can't tell you how strange it was, looking up and seeing your mother at a place like this, you know?

"So what happened was this: The cops had raided our apartment—people had complained that drug dealers were coming and going, so they came in and arrested everybody there. That's why she was at the shelter—she didn't have anyplace else to go. My mom decided it was time to turn things around. She knew she had to get off crack. And," she says, looking hard at Tanya, "she did. No programs, no clinic, no treatment, no nothing. So she had to get her act together, and she did.

"I'm real proud of her. She's changed herself a lot," Nina says proudly. "And I'm sure she's not going to have anymore relapses. She's done with that life. She's got a job here, and she's trying to save enough to get us a place. Right now she's got a voucher to stay at this one place north of the city—she gets a voucher because she's poor."

"I LIKE IT BETTER AT HARBOR LIGHTS"

"I *could* stay there, too, but I won't. I choose not to. The owner there is real sleazy, a scum lord. It's filthy, the hallways are gross,

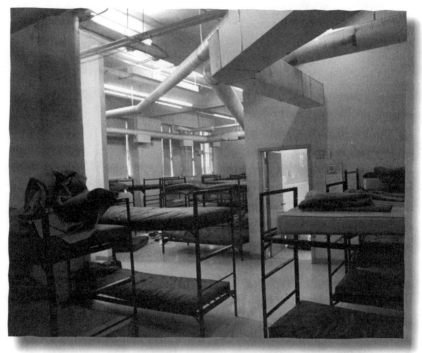

The rows of bunk beds at Harbor Lights, where Nina and her friends stay: "Me and my friends, we all try to get there right at five and get beds near each other."

the bathroom, too. It's like a boardinghouse—you share a bathroom with a lot of people. And most of the people there don't care. They're mostly alcoholics."

Instead of staying at that residence with her mother, Nina stays in a homeless shelter downtown.

"I've been staying there off and on for months," she says. "I like it better at Harbor Lights—better than staying in that place where my mom is at. It's pretty clean, and I've made some friends who are there, too."

"We're there," say Jennifer and Tanya at the same time.

AT THE SHELTER

How does it work, going to a homeless shelter on your own? Nina says it is incredibly easy.

"You just go over there at five in the afternoon," she says. "That's when it opens for the day. You go in to the front desk, sign your name, give your social security number and your birthdate, and pick your bed. Up on the third floor where we go, it's just one big room, with thirty-eight cots. You don't have to stay there until bed-time or anything—you're just claiming your bed.

"Then you have to be in by eleven on weekdays, or if it's a weekend, you can stay out till midnight. The beds are bunked—kind of like in a jail—and are made out of wire, you know what I mean? But the mattresses are pretty comfortable; they're real thick. You get clean sheets and blankets each night.

"You can't reserve the beds, even if you stay there all the time—that's just how it is. But me and my friends, we all try to get there right at five and get beds near each other. It's okay; it's not home or anything, but at least there are showers and bathrooms that are pretty clean and nobody's fighting."

"We're a Close-Knit Street Family"

Nina, Jennifer, and Tanya agree that it has helped having each other during this stressful time.

"I didn't know these guys before I started staying at Harbor Lights," Nina explains. "But they've become like sisters to me. There's a real bond among a bunch of us teenagers—and it's not just the ones at Harbor Lights, either."

Jennifer nods. "Actually, there are only about five of us that are girls, but we've got a group of about what—thirty? About thirty of us that look out for one another. We don't know each other's last names or anything, but we've gotten real close. You just see the same faces each day, eating together, standing in the same lines."

Tanya agrees. "It's been a lot easier having friends. I'm here from Illinois; I didn't know anybody at all in this city. Now I feel like I've got close friends. We're a close-knit street family."

If the family has a leader, the girls all agree, it would have to be Shirley, Nina's mother.

"She's always here, always working," Jennifer explains. "She knows everybody's name; she'll sit down and talk to anyone who needs to talk. She's 'Mom' to everybody, not just to her own daughter. That's what we call her. She's approachable and has a great personality."

"She doesn't judge us," adds Tanya. "She doesn't try to boss you, but you listen when she talks."

"I think we all get along better with guys," says Nina. "You don't have to worry about them taking your boyfriend or what-ever. Sometimes, yeah, we get romantically involved. Right now,

none of the guys in our group are around—they've all got temporary work down in St. Peter, cleaning up after the tornado. They're
gone for weeks at a time; it's good money, I guess. But I'd rather
have them around—they kind of look out for us."

PASSING THE DAYS

Nina and her friends have learned how to survive as homeless
teens in this city. Part of this survival, they say, is learning the best
places to eat for free.

"You have to leave the shelter by eight in the morning," Nina
says, fishing a cigarette out of her pocket and lighting it. "It's not

Nina is proud of the fact that she has identified the best free meals in the city.

like you can just stay in bed and sleep, even though you might really want to. But it's best, if you want a hot shower, to get up earlier than everyone else. Otherwise it's crowded, and you might not even get a shower.

"They serve breakfast there at eight, but it's not much. Usually just doughnuts and coffee. That's why we go over to the House of Charity. You can get a hot breakfast there—sausages, hash browns, eggs, toast. Sometimes they put cheese in the eggs, or onion. It's pretty good, and it opens earlier than this place."

"Yeah," says Jennifer. "We come over here mostly to check in with Mom; most of us have eaten. Sometimes, we *do* eat twice."

What about the rest of the day? What occupies their time between breakfast and their bedtime in the shelter?

"Oh, lots of stuff," says Nina. "We go to the zoo, or the park and feed the ducks. We feed the ducks a lot—just scraps of bread from lunch or breakfast. We talk, just hang out together."

Jennifer says that it's important not to loiter because police are strict about that.

"The cops don't like homeless people," she says flatly. "It's a fact. I mean, they don't even like you using the bathrooms in the department stores or anything. It seems like they know you're homeless. I know some cops recognize us—we try to stay away. Some of them are okay; but they know you're on the low end. They feel like they can harass you, call you names, whatever."

"SOMETIMES YOU JUST FEEL LIKE YOU'RE WASTING YOUR WHOLE LIFE"

Even though they have one another for support, Nina and her friends say that the homeless life is often desperately sad.

"Sometimes you just feel like you're wasting your whole life," says Nina. "Like it's all going by and you aren't moving with it. We feel sort of lost, I guess. Sometimes we just cry. You know, there's times when you have good days, but then we'll come crashing down to reality."

Jennifer sighs. "Me and Nina get together sometimes and just say, 'Man, our lives are just terrible.' But after we cry for a while, we get the tears out, and we go on. And then sometimes you just get good at covering up, too. You put on a face for everyone else."

"I try to be happy as often as I can," says Nina, smiling. "It's easier to be around other people if you at least try. And the thing is, being homeless, you almost *have* to be around other people. It's tough to be alone—in the shelters, the free dining rooms—everywhere you're with other people just like you."

"I try to take off by myself for a couple of days every so often," says Jennifer. "When I get back, all my friends have been worried about me, and I know that isn't good to do, but you really do need your time alone every once in a while. It keeps you sane."

In spite of the courageous way she approaches things, Nina admits that homelessness can be pretty sad: "Sometimes you just feel like you're wasting your whole life. . . . Sometimes we just cry."

"I Had to Grow Up Fast"

All three of the girls stress that their predicament cannot be blamed on other people; bad choices are the foundation of their homelessness.

"In my case, I shouldn't have stayed with my husband after he started using crack and being abusive," Jennifer says. "That was stupid. I rationalized it at the time; I knew he was using crack, but I figured that since I loved him so much, he couldn't stay bad. I figured I could change him. If I ignored the bad stuff—in my mind, anyway—it would be okay."

"Me, too," agrees Tanya. "I made bad choices—I think everyone does, especially when they're young—but I did learn from them. I know I won't ever do drugs again or get into trouble. I'm just looking for a way to start my life over."

Nina feels that her inability to say no to gangs, irresponsible behavior, and drug use, combined with her mother's bad choices, led to homelessness. And while it has been a very unpleasant experience, she says that homelessness has taught her some important lessons.

"I had to grow up fast," she says firmly. "Most of us did. And I've met a lot of people who think I have a lot more sense than lots of the older people that stay in the shelter. I carry myself in a way that I have some respect for myself. That's from all the mistakes I've made, and the mistakes I'm never going to make again. The thing is, I don't want to walk around like I'm a victim. That's degrading."

Looking Ahead

All three of the friends agree that looking ahead is very tempting, especially when things in the present seem bleak.

"I like to look ahead a few months," says Nina. "I think about my mom having enough money to get an apartment in a nice neighborhood. It's like we can start over, knowing so much more than we did before. And really, it's not just a fantasy—somebody owes her like three hundred dollars, so when they pay her back we'll have the deposit and the down payment.

"And when we're settled, I'd like to go back to school. I'd be a sophomore in high school. I'd like to get a part-time job and even think about college. Somewhere, a long time ago, my mom and dad started a college fund for me before I was born. I don't know if it still exists, but if it does—great!"

Nina blames bad choices on her own and her mother's plight and knows she needs to make better choices: "I don't want to walk around like I'm a victim. That's degrading."

Jennifer looks ahead to being reunited with her daughter. "I want to get myself together, get a job here," she says. "I want to bring my daughter, Evelyn, up here, and start living as a little family. Mom [Shirley] has told all of us we should give ourselves a goal of moving out of the shelter by summertime, and I'm trying.

"I had a 3.8 grade point average back in high school," she continues. "I know I'm smart enough to get a better job than a lot of other people. I want to get my act together, get going. But I want to stay connected to my street family, too. I feel like those will always be my truest friends. I have some incredible memories.

"I'll see all these guys from now on—we won't lose touch," Jennifer promises. "When I bring Evelyn up here, Nina will be her aunt. We'll always be close. We can keep each other on track when it all seems so sad."

Nina brightens. "Oh, remember that time we were all so sad and we went down to the park and started splashing around in the water? Remember? We got wet and started laughing. All of us—and we couldn't stop! I wish I'd had a camera, had pictures of those times."

"WHEN I GROW UP"

Tanya's plans for the future are very vivid. "I want to own my own nursing home," she says. "When I grow up, I mean. And I want to put a day-care nursery right in the same building. That's supposed to be healthy for the babies, healthy for the old people. And they have so much in common! Old people love babies, they like to laugh, and life doesn't give them much to smile about."

Nina frowns. "Don't you feel sorry for some of the old people in the shelters?" she asks. "Some of them are so lonely; they get all crazy from having nobody love them. I'd never want to be old and homeless—unless I could be like Grandma."

"I know," says Tanya. "Grandma is this old lady at Harbor Lights. She's really, really old. Her kids all live in town, drive nice cars and have big houses. She could live with them, but she doesn't want to. She says she's more comfortable at the shelter. All she does is read the Bible. She's read it like eighty times, I think. And she talks to you, prays for you. Everybody loves her; no one would think of hurting her. She's always saying, 'Don't worry, darling, God won't give you anything you can't handle.' But most old homeless people aren't like her."

Jennifer agrees. "There's a lot of real pitiful people we see. The ones who have given up, who don't want to work or take showers or go outside. They just sit around, smell bad, talk bad. They gave up on everything. I mean, they don't change their clothes, even though they could come here and get some for free. And there's a lot that are mentally ill. I feel sorry for them, but what can you do?"

Nina shrugs. "I know what *I'm* doing," she says. "I'm going to get out of this. Don't look for me in this place—oh, maybe two months from now. I'll be sitting in my own place with my mom. And all my friends can come over whenever they want."

Andre

"THINGS KIND OF GOT OUT OF CONTROL, AND THAT'S WHY I AIN'T BEEN HOME FOR ABOUT THREE YEARS."

Author's Note: Andre, seventeen, is personable and friendly—in fact, while I was talking with him, I had to keep reminding myself that he had been heavily involved with the drug trade in his Michigan hometown. No more, however, does he make thousands of dollars in an afternoon; he is currently flipping hamburgers at a downtown McDonald's. Like many other drug dealers his age, Andre excuses his past by saying he was desperately poor, and that he wanted to give his mother a better life. On being pressed, however, he reveals a middle-class upbringing, where both his mother and his stepfather held full-time jobs. Many of Andre's "hardships" were little more than complaints that he did not have the latest $100 basketball shoes, but had to be satisfied with last year's model. Even so, he is an engaging and likable young man, an example of what he calls the "hard-to-spot homeless."

The lady at the homeless teen center was adamant: "If you want to meet somebody interesting, you have to meet Andre. He's bright, he's articulate, and he could run for mayor—he's got so many friends!"

Andre laughs at the description. He's a smiling seventeen-year-old, wearing ragged green pants and a striped polo shirt that has clearly seen better times. He is a young man who loves to talk, and he'll be the first to admit it.

"That's about the only good thing about not having a place to live," he says. "I've got very few schedules, except the ones I want for myself. I can take my free time and just do what I want. I've got no family here, no girlfriend telling me what to do, where I've got to be. I can just be on my own, and that part isn't bad."

Andre has been homeless in this city for two months. His home-lessness is not, he says, due to a catastrophe or tragedy, as is the case with some homeless people. Instead, it has been a series of steps, each one leading farther from his family, his hometown of Saginaw, Michigan, and the life he once had.

"ONE OF THOSE HARD-TO-SPOT HOMELESS"

"I'm one of those hard-to-spot homeless people," Andre explains. "I don't fit the image most people have of a homeless guy. I'm not crazy—at least not yet," he grins. "And I don't sleep on park benches or in shelters. I've done that—even the park benches, once or twice, but now I don't even sleep in a shelter. I'm sleeping in the apartment of this guy I work with—he and his mother Sharon have this place. So I get to sleep on the couch, and that's pretty nice. And yeah, I have a job. That's the other thing that doesn't sound right for a homeless guy, huh? I've got a job working at McDonald's downtown.

"Anyway, I have a couch to sleep on for a few weeks," he says. "And I've got a little job. But I've got nowhere to be. I've got no place to put my stuff, or hang out when I'm not working. I line up at 6:30 in the morning with a bunch of other guys outside this one place run by Catholic Charities if I want to take a hot shower. They've also got some lockers where I can keep some of my stuff—like my winter coat and a couple extra pairs of pants. That helps a lot.

"I hang out at this teen center for runaways and other homeless kids in the evening. I can eat there, watch a little television. I don't really feel comfortable going to my friend's apartment except late at night to sleep. It's not my place, so I feel funny, you know? And when I leave there, I'm not sure where I'll go."

FROM MICHIGAN

Andre is from Michigan originally; he has lived in both Detroit and Saginaw.

"At first I was living in Saginaw," he says. "It was my mother and me. My dad—I don't really know him. He and my mother were never married or nothing. He wasn't there for me. So it was me and my mother for a while.

"We lived in a pretty bad part of the city—I guess you could really say it was the ghetto. We had a house, a nice little three-bedroom. My mother worked construction with my uncle, doing dry wall, painting, roofing, stuff like that. She went to college—to a community college—to learn how to do it, I guess. And we weren't really poor because my father sent child support. He had a good job in the Cadillac plant in Detroit, I think."

Andre says that even though his own family was not poor, the neighborhood was very bleak.

"It was real run-down," he says. "Lots of dope selling going on. Lots of people getting killed over nothing, like basketball games or

Andre reads at the public library: "I'm one of those hard-to-spot homeless people. I don't fit the image most people have of a homeless guy."

dice games. It was hard seeing that. Growing up there, I saw a lot. I know I was pretty little when I figured that where I lived wasn't so good."

He snaps his fingers, remembering.

"Oh, I'll tell you what. I remember when me and three of my friends were about nine years old. We went over to the park to play basketball. The park had like a concession stand, you know? And there was a bathroom attached to it. Well, we went in the bathroom, and we kept smelling this foul odor, really bad.

"And I'm like, 'Man, that smells like somebody died in here or something.' We were all laughing and everything. Then we opened the stall door, and there was this dead body. This man was sitting there. He'd been dead a couple of days, I guess—strangled, I think. We were so scared! I didn't throw up or nothing because I have a real strong stomach. My friends, they got kind of green, and they ran out faster than I did. When I got home I told my mother and she called the police."

A NEW BROTHER

Andre ranks his mother as the sweetest, kindest person he's ever known. However, he says, smiling, she has her ups and downs.

"Like anybody, I guess," he says. "I wish she was with me now. I really do. I know right now she's going through some of the same stuff I am. But you know what? I haven't seen her in a real long time—since I was fourteen. So even though I talk about her like we were real close, I can't say that we were close the last year or so I was home. Things kind of got out of control, and that's why I ain't been home for about three years.

"It was me and my mom, just the two of us, until I was about ten years old. And then one day, out of the clear blue sky, she tells me I'm going to have a little brother. I was jealous, man."

Andre smiles broadly. "I knew that once that baby was born I wasn't going to have my mother to myself no more. Once he got here, though, he was okay. She named him De Lawrence, after his father, who was called Larry. He was the cutest little thing, I've got to admit. Now, me and De Lawrence have different fathers. But Larry—he was like a father to me, more than my real father was."

HAPPY TIMES

Andre says that he was often the baby-sitter of choice, but it didn't interfere too much with his life.

"My mother, she's a bingo *fiend*," he laughs. "When she ain't working, she loves to play her bingo. So me and De Lawrence, we'd kind of hang during the day. He wasn't any trouble, either. He really liked me—I could lay down with him for like five minutes, and then he'd be asleep. Then I could go out and play with my friends. See, my job was to get him to sleep—then my cousin or somebody who was around, they'd stay around and listen for him, in case he woke up. But when he woke up, it was usually me he was looking for."

Without a doubt, he says, those times—spent with his mother, Larry, and little De Lawrence—make up his happiest childhood memories.

"We did a lot together," he says. "Every chance we got, me and Larry would plan a fishing trip. We'd go up to the Detroit River or to this little place called Strawberry Lake. Man, the water was so clear, you could see all the way to the bottom! We'd catch bluegills, crappies, sunfish—sometimes even a walleye, when they were running.

"We'd take the little barbeque grill out there with us and eat what we caught. My mom and De Lawrence would come. My mom would sometimes fish, too. And De Lawrence—his main job was to help scare the fish away," he laughs.

DOWNSLIDING

Things started going sour for Andre when he was about thirteen.

"For one thing, school started getting bad," he says, frowning. "I'll tell you, I'm pretty smart. I kept up a 2.89 grade point average; I always did my homework when I was supposed to in grade school. But then in junior high everything got boring. It seemed like we were always learning the same things over and over. It was for all the new kids, I think—or the dumb kids who didn't get it.

"But man, I was tired of hearing it. Math, reading, whatever—it was repetitive. See, as far as I'm concerned, if I tell you that I already learned something, and it says on my report card that I got an A or a B last year when I learned it, or I can prove that I know it by taking some test or other, then why do you make me sit there and learn it again? That was so stupid! I took it this way—the teachers were disrespecting me, making me sit through it all again."

Andre sighs. "I started getting into trouble pretty bad then. Back then I was always mad at my mother. It seemed like she was so strict! Way stricter than any of the other mothers around my neighborhood. I mean, I used to be inside, doing my chores, doing my homework, and I could look outside and see my friends all out there playing. They were playing basketball, playing with the girls, just having fun. And I used to really feel angry that she wasn't letting me have that same freedom as my friends got, you know? So after a while, I guess I did something about it."

"IT WAS EASY"

Andre is reluctant to say just what it is that he did. He shrugs and smiles, trying to change the subject. Eventually he draws a deep breath and nods.

"Okay, so this is what I did. I started doing what everyone else in my neighborhood was doing. I started selling dope. I mean, I wasn't a pusher or nothing. I'd buy the dope—the cocaine—and I'd cook it and have somebody else sell the crack for me. I'd get the powder for like a thousand dollars at a time.

"Yeah, I was thirteen, fourteen—I don't know. I am not defending this—I'm telling you this was a case of me standing up for myself against my mother. I rebelled, I guess. I got started doing it, just like all my friends did. Fact is, I don't think I remember any of my friends from when I was eight or nine that weren't doing dope selling by the time they were thirteen. It's just the way the neighborhood was."

Andre refuses to say exactly how he was able to procure a thousand dollars of cocaine the first time, or how he knew the correct "recipe" for making crack cocaine. He only says that it was extremely easy.

"I wasn't a big genius," he says. "I was in like seventh grade, you know? I'm telling you it was easy. I wouldn't cook it in my own kitchen, no. See, a lot of my friends' mothers smoked crack. My mother didn't, but her friends did. And they knew I was selling. They'd never tell my mother, no, because they'd lose their easy supply. They'd let me use their kitchen, and in exchange, I'd give them some of my crack, as soon as it was done.

"The rest of it I'd bag up and give to somebody to sell. And it was lots of money—lots. I made a ton of money—didn't even think about how much it was. It just came rolling in. I probably could have made more, but it seemed like as long as I was getting enough to have fun with, I was pretty happy."

SPENDING MONEY

Andre spent his money casually, he remembers, and unselfishly.

"I didn't really think about how much I was spending at the time," he says, with more than a hint of boasting. "I'd go out with my four best friends—we'd rent a car from somebody in the neighborhood, and we'd go to the mall. I'd buy everybody outfits, nice clothes to wear. I'd buy expensive things for my girlfriend, for her friends, too. We'd go out to eat, and I'd pay.

Andre window-shops at a clothing store. When he was selling drugs, he had the money to purchase anything that he wanted.

"I used to give my mom money sometimes, like if we were at the grocery store and she needed extra. She'd say, 'Hey, Andre, give me twenty dollars; I'll pay you back when we get home.' I'd give it to her but I'd never mention it when we got home. I sometimes would surprise them, too—I'd get lobster or steak or something from some restaurant and bring it home."

Andre says that his parents assumed the money came from his summer job.

"It was this little job through the school system there," he says. "I'd go to school in the summer, for three hours, and then I'd go to work three hours. The work wasn't too hard, just cleaning up school buildings and stuff like that. And I'd get paid $215 each week."

He smiles. "Nice money, huh?"

SHE DIDN'T WANT TO ASK, BUT SHE KNEW

At first, Andre says, his mother had no idea how much money he was making.

"I was socking most of it away," he shrugs. "I'd use a thousand dollars or so for my next batch of powder and keep the rest in my room. What I did was, I hid it in my mattress. It got so that there wasn't enough room in that old mattress for the cotton that was *supposed* to be in there!

"So one day she was cleaning my room, and she found a hole in the mattress. She says to me, 'Where'd this hole come from?' I didn't know what to say, so I told her I didn't know. She stuck her hand in there and started pulling out wads of money. I just kept looking at her face as she was pulling that money out. She says, 'You're sleeping on money, Andre.' And I was. There was at least twenty-five thousand dollars in there, probably more. I was just sleeping on it."

His mother didn't ask where the money came from.

"My mother was not stupid; I'm thinking that nine times out of ten when my mom guessed about something, she guessed right," he says. "I figure since she didn't ask me, she didn't want to hear it. My mother is the type of person, if she asks you a direct question and you lie, she won't let up till the truth is out. But she didn't ask me a direct question.

"What she did was, she told me it wasn't safe to keep that much money in the house. She took some, put it in the bank under her name, then some under my stepfather's name, and some in my

Andre waits for the public bus. When Andre's mother discovered he was selling drugs, she didn't have the usual maternal reaction. Instead of telling him to stop, she told him, "Whatever you decide to do in this world, Andre, you make sure you be the best at it."

grandmother's bank account. She didn't tell me anything like 'Don't do it no more.' I think she figured that having that much money, I was used to that life. Telling me not to do it anymore wouldn't have done any good. What she said was, 'Whatever you decide to do in this world, Andre, you make sure you be the best at it; don't be no dummy at what you do.'"

Andre tilts his head and smiles. "I took that affirmation, and I used it," he says.

Andre's life in Saginaw revolved around drugs and the money he made from them. School and family slipped further and further from his mind.

"I wasn't spending much time in school," he admits. "I skipped for a whole year, in fact—never got caught. Sometimes I didn't even go; sometimes I'd just go and hang out in the hall and not go to class at all. The way I skipped for a year was this: I just never gave out our phone number on that form you've got to fill out at the beginning of the year.

"They couldn't call. And when they sent letters, I was there to intercept them before my mother or Larry came home from work. See, school got out at 2:35, and I was home by 2:50 at the latest— I'd beat the mailman home. Anything that came with the school's name on the envelope—I'd destroy it fast."

"I WAS TIRED OF SEEING MY MAMA STRUGGLE"

Life for Andre as a fourteen-year-old boy in Michigan was about making money. But didn't he feel guilty, knowing what he did was illegal? Didn't he think about the people whose lives were being destroyed by the drugs he was concocting in other people's kitchens? Andre frowns.

"I didn't think of it that way," he says. "What can I tell you? The way I looked at things was this: I was tired of seeing my mama struggle; that's why I got into all of this. It was just hard watching her struggle to survive."

But Andre's mother had a good job doing construction, and his stepfather had a full-time job as a custodian. Compared to most of their neighbors, they must have been doing quite well. When asked how they struggled, Andre looks cornered.

"Well," he says uncertainly, "We always had new stuff—new cars, bills. We had mortgage payments. She was living on a budget, you know? And that was hard.

"Besides," he continues, now annoyed, "I got tired of us settling for second best. Like when I wanted new basketball shoes, you know—Jordans or some good kind—I was never able to get the new Jordans. I got last year's Jordans, the ones that were out of date. I basically got tired of settling for that. I wanted the best for my mother and my stepfather."

Even as he says these words, Andre realizes that he has contradicted himself, and he is annoyed and embarrassed. He is ready to talk about something other than his drug dealing, he says.

THE FIRST STEPS AWAY FROM HOME

How did he go from being a wealthy drug dealer to working for minimum wage in another city? Andre explains that it happened in stages, but the very first part was when he wanted to go to a party.

"I was sort of leading a double life," he says. "I was still trying to be home when my mother was; I didn't want her mad at me because she was scary when she got mad! I hung around with De Lawrence and asked permission to go out, same as I used to.

"But this time when I wanted to go out, she told me that I had to be back at midnight. But it was already after nine, and I knew that it wasn't enough time to have fun. So I promised her I'd be home, but really I'd gotten some clothes out of my room and threw them out the window. I went outside, grabbed my clothes, and went to my friend Kendrick's house. I dropped off the clothes and went to my girlfriend's house.

"Well, one thing led to another, and I stayed the night at her house. And the next morning I went over to Kendrick's, and he told me my mother had been there looking for me, and she was mad. I asked him what he'd told her. He said, 'I told her you were at your little girlfriend's house.' I asked him what my mother said then. He told me, 'She said you better get your butt home right now because you were supposed to be home last night at midnight.' Well, I knew what was in store for me if I went home; I'd get a whupping. And my mom believed in whuppings until *she* got tired! So I just stayed at Kendrick's."

Andre stayed a week, then another week. Kendrick's mother was almost never home, so he was not forced to explain his presence.

"My mama showed up every once in a while at first," he says. "One time she was at the front door when we were going out the back. She was worried at first, I guess. But then she'd run into my friends, and they'd tell her, 'Oh, no, nothing's wrong with Andre, he's fine. But we haven't seen him.'"

Andre laughs. "I'm sure she was mad. And now, when I look back, I know I should have gone right home with her because she was trying to raise me the best she could. And if I'd listened, I know I wouldn't be here now, that's a fact. I was trying to be a big man, trying to be like everybody else. I should have been myself, instead of messing around like some of them boys. But that's history, man."

FINDING ANTHONY'S STASH

After a few weeks his mother stopped looking for him, realizing that he would come home when he was ready.

"But you know what?" he says. "I ain't seen her since that night when she told me to be in by midnight. See, I started living over there at Kendrick's, and I was living the high life. I had my own money, and nothing much changed, except I had a lot more freedom, and I didn't have to do no lying to my mother.

"But then something happened. Kendrick's brother Anthony was a dope dealer, you know? He did a lot of business, and Kendrick found his stash one day—like I had my mattress. Well, Anthony was using the pipe of this old heater that wasn't connected up on the second floor. The money was just in there, stacks of it. At first I didn't know about the money. All I knew was that Kendrick had a lot of money; he'd be taking me to the mall and buying me stuff. He was taking like five or six thousand dollars at a time!

"I'd say, 'Hey, I've got my own money, you don't need to be buying me clothes.' But he'd just laugh and say not to worry about it. So that went on a while. Then one day I came upstairs, and he had all this money lying on a little table. It was more than I'd seen since I had all that stash in my mattress—and that money was in everybody else's bank account but mine.

"So I told him, 'Hey, Kendrick, you've got to give me some of that money. I don't want any clothes; I want half of that money.' So he gave me half and took half for himself."

CAUGHT

Andre and Kendrick weren't particularly worried about being discovered stealing from Anthony. The older boy was, says Andre, pretty slow.

"He wasn't like retarded or anything," he says. "I mean, he could count and read and stuff. If you gave him a stack of a hundred one-dollar bills, he could count them right and put them back in his pocket, but after a few minutes he'd sort of forget how much he'd counted. He just didn't remember real good.

When Andre got in trouble with other drug dealers, his mother sent him to live with an uncle, which changed his perspective: "I didn't get mad at people as easy, when things didn't go my way."

"So this went on for a couple months; we'd take a bunch of his money and split it. But then one day we got caught. See, we found a stash that Anthony had set aside for getting his car fixed. It was in a new hiding place, under the carpet. We should have known he'd remember the exact amount—since it had to do with his car, I guess. We took money once too often—I guess we were being pretty greedy. And since he'd never gotten suspicious, we didn't figure we had to worry.

"But he was mad. He came downstairs and pulled a pistol on us. He said, 'You all are going to pay me back, every penny of what you took.' We were scared, but we didn't think he'd really shoot. But he was so mad; he told us that even if we had to steal money, we had to pay him back. I think in a way he was kind of hurt. See, he'd always been nice to us, let us drive his car sometimes, and he'd give us a little money when we were younger. So he felt like we betrayed him or whatever."

"JUST LIKE FRESH PRINCE OF BEL-AIR"

Andre knew that he had little choice but to pay back his share of what he and Kendrick stole. He also knew that he didn't have enough money to pay back the full amount.

"I didn't want to mess with any of Anthony's friends or whatever," he says. "I mean, Anthony's dealers might come looking for us, and they didn't have any loyalty to either me or Kendrick. So I called my mother and told her what had happened.

"This was the first time I'd talked to her in a long time—since I left home. She was mad! She was like, 'Oh, now you're calling, now that you need money. It's been all summer, and now you decide you need to talk to me, now that you got dangerous people trying to kill you if you don't give them their money.' I tried explaining that Anthony wouldn't hurt me, but she wouldn't listen.

"Then she said that she was going to send me away. I was almost fifteen years old, she said, and I wasn't learning how to stay out of trouble. You know about that show, *Fresh Prince*—how they sent him away. That's what she was going to do, send me away from my neighborhood, just like Fresh Prince of Bel-Air. Except I was going to live with my uncle and auntie in Detroit."

Andre says that he told her he didn't want to go, but his protests fell on deaf ears.

"She said that either I went or I had to stay there in Saginaw and get my butt whupped by those drug dealers. Either way, she wasn't going to give me any money. She didn't care that all my friends were in Saginaw, all my life was there. She packed up my clothes, and my uncle came to get me."

A DIFFERENT LIFE

It was a different life in Detroit. Andre had no access to enough money to start his drug business again, even if he had wanted to. He went to school and was given a part-time job.

"I didn't have a lot of choice, I guess," he says. "They kept track of me, so I couldn't skip school like I'd done back home. And my uncle's house was right behind this little corner store, so that's where I worked. I swept up, did the bottles, cleaned windows, whatever had to be done. It was a big adjustment, that's for sure!

"One thing that really changed for me is that I didn't feel so angry all the time. I guess I was mad a lot back in Saginaw, but I didn't realize it. But once I got away from all the stuff going on in Saginaw, I felt better. I was more relaxed, I guess. I also learned to control the anger I had inside. What I'd do is this: I'd sit in my room, just by myself. And I'd just sort of meditate. I know that sounds kind of funny, but it's what I did. I just closed the door and sat on the bed and told myself, don't get mad, don't get mad. That's how I changed myself."

Andre says that in his new surroundings he was a much more even-tempered person.

"I felt different," he admits. "For one thing, I had to spend more time with myself than I ever had before. So I guess to survive that, I had to be easier to get along with. I didn't get mad at people as easy, when things didn't go my way."

A VACATION

Andre had an uncle who was living in Minneapolis, and he invited Andre to come for a visit. Trusting her nephew to make the trip alone, his aunt in Detroit gave her permission.

"It was exciting, coming here," he says. "I'd heard about it, but I didn't think I'd get a chance to see it. So I came up here to see the sights, get to know my uncle better. But what happened was this: A few days after I got here, he got word from my father—you know, he works in the Cadillac plant? Well, my father tells my uncle that he can get a job in the plant there, and my uncle is all excited.

"Next thing I know, he's packing his stuff up, and is getting the two of us bus tickets to go back to Michigan. But I'm like, 'Hey, I'm not ready to go! I've met some people, and I'm just starting to have fun.' So he thinks about it and decides that I can finish out the rest of the month at his apartment, since the rent is paid up anyway. And he leaves my bus ticket at the bus station, so I can come back home."

His uncle also left him a little cash for food, Andre says. At first, Andre felt very grown-up living on his own in the city; however, after two and a half weeks, that heady feeling ended.

"I came home late one night," he remembers, "and there was a note on the door. It said, 'Pay next month's rent or clear out and leave the key.' Well, paying the rent was out of the question since all the cash my uncle left me was gone. But I didn't want to go back to Detroit, either. So I just cleared out my stuff and left."

ON THE STREETS

Andre says that he went from being a vacationer to a sort of "volunteer" homeless teen very quickly.

"See, at first being homeless didn't really bother me," he says. "I knew a few people, I figured I could find a place to stay or something. But it wasn't like that. Nobody really had a place for me to stay; nobody had room. And I didn't have much money at all—that got used up fast for food.

"I went to shelters at first. Just a bed for the night, and then you clear out. You can take showers down at the Branch—that's run by the Catholic Church, like I told you before. You've got to line up early, like seven in the morning if you want a shower. And then they've got a soup line—pretty good breakfasts, usually."

He found out within several days that there is a center for homeless and runaway teens in town, and he went there frequently.

"You can't sleep there, but it's open in the afternoon and evening," he says. "They can hook you up with a counselor if you've got stuff to talk about, and you get a meal. Plus there's just a place to hang out—they've got couches and a TV and stuff, so you don't have to be spending your days in the library or hanging around in doorways like the winos."

DAYDREAMING

Staying in shelters and eating in soup kitchens was not something Andre wanted to do on a long-term basis—especially after having enjoyed a much wealthier lifestyle.

"I used to think about that, standing in line for a shower," he said. "Or getting a bus token so I could get around. I'd think about how much money I used to have. I don't mean that I wanted to be selling drugs now, but man, the money sure was fine.

"Did I tell you I had a car back when I was fifteen?" he asks, with more than a hint of boastfulness in his voice. "Actually, I had more than one. It was easy, even though I was too young to get a license. See, as long as you've got the money, you can get pretty

Andre quickly realized that being homeless was not easy: "Nobody really had a place for me to stay. . . . And I didn't have much money at all—that got used up fast for food."

near everything you want in my neighborhood. You don't go to a dealer—no. You just find someone who wants to sell a car. I had me a '78 Cutlass, a black one. Then I had a blue one that I had painted midnight blue. And my last one was yellow; I got it painted white.

"I was smart enough to take the cars to one of my stepfather's friends—put the title in his name. And as long as I just drove around the neighborhood I was fine. If we were going outside, I'd just have one of my older friends drive.

"So anyway, I'd think about that when I was homeless. I'd think about that mattress full of money. I used to say to myself, 'Man, Andre, you sure do have your ups and downs!'"

GETTING A JOB

Andre found himself in a McDonald's one day at the noon rush and was amazed at how inefficient it seemed.

"I was so hungry," he smiles. "And it was so slow! There were only like two people behind the counter and all these people standing in line. I'm like, 'Man, you've got to get some help back there—people are getting mad. This isn't a fast-food place—this is *slow* food!' So the manager kind of laughs and pulls out an application form for me. I filled it out right there, and he hired me right on the spot!

"Now I've been there three weeks. It's a great place; I met some nice people there. I know some people would say that it's a chump job, you know, flipping burgers or whatever. And I know that back in Saginaw I was making more money in about twenty minutes than I do working a couple days here. But nobody's going to throw me in jail for working there, you know? That's the difference.

"I'm not making too much—only $6.15 an hour. But I can eat there, and it's something to do. I'm trying to save up, maybe get my own place sometime. At first I was going from the shelter to work, trying to do that—but it was hard. I was talking to my manager at work one day, talking about my situation, and this one guy I work with overheard.

"That's the one who said I could camp out at his place with him and his mother. So like I told you, I'm doing that for a while. Not too long. And I still am hanging out at the center in the evenings after work. I don't want to be in my friend's apartment for too long. I can't relax there. You've got to be polite or talk when you don't feel like talking. I don't like that because you can never feel like just being yourself. But I don't want to sound like I'm complaining because I'm real grateful they let me sleep there. It would be hard working and staying in a shelter, I think.

"The funny thing is feeling like a regular person, you know, during the day when I'm working. Then when everyone else goes home, back to their lives, I've got nothing. I never could have believed before that you could be employed and still be homeless!"

"I'VE BEEN ON MY OWN A LOT"

Andre says that he has stayed in touch with his relatives in Michigan, including his mother.

"At first they were kind of upset, especially my uncle who used to live here," he says. "He talked to me, tried to get me to come home. But now I really can't. I don't feel like I can. I'm here, and I'm trying to get on my feet. See, they feel guilty because I'm underage. They don't think I should be on my own.

Andre works hard at his job at McDonald's. "I know some people would say that it's a chump job. . . . But nobody's going to throw me in jail for working there, you know?"

"But I told them, I've been on my own a lot in my life. Basically, I've been on my own since I left my mother's house when I was fourteen. So just because I'm in a different city, it's not a big deal. It's just not having the money that's hard.

"The sooner I get myself established, the better it's going to be for me down the line. If I wait to get on my own, what am I waiting for? I dropped out of school back in Detroit when I turned sixteen. I'm not going to get any smarter, except maybe street smart.

Andre does not feel bad about having no adults to take care of him: "Basically, I've been on my own since I left my mother's house when I was fourteen."

And I'm not going to get any richer than I used to be—probably never *as rich* as I used to be."

Andre laughs. "I've got a job, and I'm getting things figured out. I'm a strong-minded person; I don't want any trouble in my life. I had enough of that. I carried a gun back in Saginaw. I had people shooting at me sometimes. I don't need to have all that drama in my life any more. I guess the only drama I've got going on is working. And I've got nothing else to do with my time, so I might as well work."

MISSING HIS MOTHER

Andre admits that he gets lonely—especially for his mother and little brother.

"I know that sounds phony," he says, "but it's true. My mama and I have had some nice talks on the phone. She's had a lot of changes in her life lately; she's not married to Larry anymore. It's just her and De Lawrence.

"Man, that boy is *smart!*" he says proudly. "He's going to be eight next January, and he's a real little brainiac. He gets all kinds of awards in school. Last year he entered a spelling bee and got third in the whole city! I talk to him on the phone sometimes. I want him to stay like he is, though—not start running with punks. It's harder for me because I don't have much education. But De Lawrence will have lots of choices, he can do whatever he wants.

"My mama is talking more and more about coming up here to live. She wants to get De Lawrence out of that city; she's worried about what happens in that neighborhood. And I'd really like it if she came here."

Would he move back in with his mother if she did make her home here? Andre looks uncertain.

"I don't think so," he admits. "I really mean it when I say I'm trying to grow up, to be a man. I don't want to go through all this and then feel like I'm moving back home with my mother. That's like taking a step backwards, you know? I'd like to visit her, see her every day. But not live there. I feel too old for that. I know I'm only seventeen. But some days, I feel like I'm really old."

Athena

"I'VE LIVED OUTSIDE SO LONG—
UNDER BRIDGES, IN THE PARK,
YOU NAME IT—I SOMETIMES FEEL
LIKE I'M GOING TO SCREAM WHEN
I'M INSIDE. BUT I'M GIVING IT A
CHANCE. AND HOPEFULLY SOON
I'LL FEEL STRONGER ABOUT BEING
OUT ON MY OWN."

Author's Note: Of all the homeless teens I talked to in the course of writing this book, nineteen-year-old Athena is the most interesting and the most honest. What youth workers would term a "throwaway," Athena comes from a broken home; her parents divorced when she was five. Her mother wanted nothing to do with Athena and her brother and proceeded to marry what Athena terms "a whole string of alcoholics, one after another." Athena lived instead with her father, who was physically and emotionally abusive.

Athena's young life has been filled with beatings, substance abuse, foster care, and life on the streets. She is quick to point out her own failures and mistakes, too—rejecting the idea of being "poor little Athena." She is gay and prides herself on being strong—in her words, "a true survivor." Homeless until just recently, Athena has ended her drug use and is currently in transitional housing aimed at at-risk young people.

"I've been off the streets for a little while now," Athena laughs. "But you'd think I was still homeless. I eat like a homeless person—one meal a day. I sit down when I can and *whooooosh!* I just inhale any kind of food I can find. And then I don't eat again until the next day. It's like being a camel, except with food instead of water!"

Nineteen-year-old Athena would have trouble blending into a crowd. She is dressed in a tank top and camouflage pants and wears steel-toed boots. Her bleached hair stands up in stiff spikes. When she smiles—which is often—you can see a flash of silver, a bright stud in the middle of her tongue. She also sports a silver ring in her left nostril and has a tattoo proclaiming "Girls" on her left forearm.

"IT'S ME AND ED RIGHT NOW"

She is proud of herself for accomplishing what a year ago would have seemed impossible: ending both her reliance on drugs, especially crystal meth (a particularly powerful form of speed), and her homelessness.

"I'm queer," she says, smiling. "I'm in a program called Host Home, which pairs gay kids between the ages of eighteen and twenty-one with gay adults. The kids are like me—on the edge, formerly homeless who are trying to get their feet on solid ground. Many of us—me included—have had bad experiences in the foster care or treatment systems—being queer is a real handicap in many cases. It's like one more strike against you, you know. So by getting paired with someone who knows what it's like, it removes that sense of being an outsider, I guess you could say.

"I'm paired with this guy named Ed," she explains. "He's a hairdresser. He's also a writer; he's writing his—I don't know—third novel, maybe? It's called *White-Out*, and it's supposed to be about the annihilation of the white race."

She grins. "So it's me and Ed right now, just the two of us. I'm not sure if it's the best matchup, but we're trying. To tell you the truth, the house where he lives is so nice, I feel really out of my element. I've lived outside so long—under bridges, in the park, you name it—I sometimes feel like I'm going to scream when I'm inside. But I'm giving it a chance. And hopefully soon I'll feel stronger about being out on my own."

NOT MANY GOOD MEMORIES

Athena's smile fades a bit when asked about her family. She admits that she doesn't have many good memories growing up.

"I was born in West Germany, actually," she begins. "My dad was in the army, and we lived on army bases all over the place. We were in Italy for a while—that's where my brother, Adam, was born. And I've lived in Texas, South Korea, Virginia, and Maryland.

Athena talks with Ed, a man who participates in a program called Host Home, and has agreed to give Athena a place to stay. "I'm not sure if its the best matchup, but we're trying," says Nina frankly.

"I don't remember a lot when I was little. One thing I remember in Italy was this guy across the street; he had the biggest birdcage you could imagine. I used to walk inside it and talk to the birds. And the man would go, 'Sshhh! You'll scare them.' That's about it for Italian memories—the good ones, at least."

Athena says most of her family memories are painful ones.

"My parents fought a lot," she says. "My dad used to rape my mom; he had all kinds of aggressive problems. And my mom was an alcoholic, so she had her own set of things going on. I remember hearing the screaming, the thuds in the next room. At the time I was too young to know what was going on, but it was explained to me when I got older. It wasn't a very big secret, really.

"They got divorced when we moved to Maryland. My mom lost custody of my brother and me—she didn't seem very interested in having us live with her. She never showed up when she was allowed to visit. So, I guess we got the message pretty quick, right?" She laughs, a rueful smile on her face.

"I'M NOT TALKING ABOUT SPANKINGS, HERE"

Her growing-up years were spent with her brother, her father, and his new wife, Helen.

"She was in the army, too—and she outranked my father, which was kind of funny," says Athena. "He is a major, she's a lieutenant colonel. He didn't rape her—Helen was a pretty tough lady. My dad used to hit us a lot; after my mom left he really laid into us. But he did plenty of it back when they were still married, too. And I'm not talking about spankings, here—I'm talking about getting thrown across the room, getting smacked with fists and belts. Just getting pounded.

"I remember once when we were living in Italy; I was like two or three, being potty trained. I had an accident on the kitchen floor. He got so mad he pounded the shit out of me, just beat me. My mom had to kick him out of the house and he slept in the car that night. It was really scary—our dog was so frightened he went after my dad. I guess he thought it was a life and death thing."

Her father beat her brother, too, but he seemed to save most of his aggression for Athena.

"I was the one he would vent on when he had a bad day," she says. "The thing was, he had no expectations about me; he didn't care about me at all. I was his safety valve, only good for being a target, I guess. Now, Adam—he had high expectations of my brother. He had to be perfect. I used to hear arguments about Adam being in Boy Scouts. Adam didn't want to join, but when he mentioned that to my dad, he'd get beaten. My dad would say things like, 'You're going to be an Eagle Scout or else.' So Adam had no choice, really.

"I found out later that my mom had wanted to leave long before she actually did—I guess that makes sense. She told me later that she had to leave when we moved to Maryland for mental health reasons. Adam and I used to sort of laugh about that, like, okay— so he was beating the crap out of you, what made you think he wasn't going to beat the crap out of us when you left? I mean, she knew he hit us all the time. It wasn't like he hid it from her. But I guess she was just looking out for herself. That was all she was capable of doing."

Athena's father beat her from the time she was a small child: "I was the one he would vent on when he had a bad day. . . . I was his safety valve, only good for being a target."

"ATHENA'S IN THE BASEMENT; THE REAL FAMILY IS UPSTAIRS"

Athena says that her mother had almost no contact with her or Adam as they grew up, and her father used that rejection to hurt them.

"He'd say things like, 'Hey, no wonder your mom doesn't want you,' to us, and it would really make me feel terrible," she recalls. "I remember feeling that I was so different from other kids, even from kids of divorced parents because even the noncustodial parent would visit or see them on holidays. With my mom it was nothing—maybe a call once a year or something.

"I think for a long time I coped by making up big fantasies about my mother. I'd tell people she lived in England and had a horse." Athena laughs. "I just totally lied because I wanted the situation to be cool. I didn't want anyone to pity me—I didn't want anybody to even know what was really going on. How can a kid admit to someone that their mother had voluntarily, you know, left?"

Her relationship with her father was hardly a comfort, either.

"I remember feeling shunned a lot," she admits. "I've been told since that because I resemble my mother, maybe that was the cause of my father's disinterest in me. I felt really cut off, though, from that family. I had a room in the basement with no windows. I wasn't even allowed up on the second floor where everyone else's bedrooms were. My dad told me I had no business up there, there was no need for me to go upstairs. It was like, 'Athena's in the basement; the real family is upstairs.'

A MYSTERY TO OTHER PEOPLE

Outside of the family, Athena was something of a mystery. In the neighborhood, she was often a bully; in school she was very quiet.

"I picked on younger kids, older kids—it didn't seem to matter," she shrugs, a little embarrassed. "I hung out with mostly boys; I started drinking. By the time I was twelve I was smoking pot, using morphine that a neighborhood kid was able to get, and even using some acid.

"But in school, I didn't say much. I was an okay student—I did real well in English and artsy things. I couldn't do math or science at all. And I remember my teachers being very concerned when I hit sixth grade because Adam and I were in the same school. They thought *I* was quiet! Adam never spoke a word!

"Even at home, he wouldn't talk. He wasn't mad or anything—he just didn't want people talking to him. He had no friends at all; I remember him sitting at home in his room, building things out of Legos and Construx. He'd build the most awesome things, and then he'd run downstairs to the basement and get me to come see what he'd made. Then he'd destroy whatever it was before anyone else could see."

This memory makes Athena sad. "Adam was such a nice little boy," she says quietly.

Locked Up and Sent Away

When she was thirteen, Athena overdosed on amphetamines. She had been using drugs with increasing frequency—but never with friends, always alone.

"When I OD'd, I got sent to this treatment facility especially for juvenile delinquents with chronic or terminal illnesses," she says. "I guess there was a lot of evidence to suggest that kids who had no control over their health sometimes acted out really badly. I had diabetes—that's why I qualified.

"So I was there for three months. And actually it was sort of enjoyable for me. I felt really safe there; there was no hitting, no yelling. There had been so much of that, you see. Anyway, afterwards my dad made it really clear that they didn't want me back. So the counselors decided—in their wisdom—to place me with my mom, who lived up here. I wasn't sure how I felt about it—I guess I felt like I didn't really know her. But she had agreed to take me. I figured, she's my mom—how bad could it be?

"It was awful," she says. "Really awful. She was remarried, and her husband was a real jerk. He made it clear he didn't want kids around. He'd walk around the house completely naked and that grossed me out. I tried talking to my mom about it, and she was like, 'Hey, it's his house; you should feel lucky that he's even allowing you to stay here. Nobody wants you at your dad's.'"

Athena shakes her head. "It sounded real familiar," she says. "So what happened was, he started getting real abusive. He threw a beer bottle so hard it embedded in the wall just inches above my head when I was sitting on the couch. And he burned me with his cigarette—see?"

She points to a round scar on her hand. "That's for not moving fast enough when he told me to get him his cigarettes," she explains.

In the System

After the bottle-throwing incident, Athena was so frightened that she ran outside and hopped on a bicycle to get away.

"It had two flat tires," she says, smiling. "It was not the best transportation I could have hoped for. But I pedaled and pedaled—I didn't know where I was going. I'd only been here for two weeks; I just kept pedaling. I went quite a distance, too—all the way to

Athena's teen years were spent in and out of shelters and foster homes and, finally, a stint with her father: "The devil you know is better than the devil you don't. I knew what to expect at my dad's."

Hugo. I got to a diner or whatever—went inside and ran to the bathroom. I just sat there, crying as hard as I've ever cried in my whole life.

"A waitress there called the cops. I guess she was freaked because she'd never seen anybody crying in the bathroom before. So they came and got me. They took me to this center for runaways and other kinds of offenders located in St. Paul. I stayed there for a while—I did okay. Nobody wanted me back—not my mom, not my dad. Then I was told I was getting placed with this foster family. So after hearing that," she says, lighting a cigarette and blowing out the match, "I got happy feet and left."

She ended up going back, however, after she tried to get a bed at a youth shelter.

"I told them my name," she says, "and I guess on the computer or whatever, I had something next to my name that showed I was on the run. So the police came and brought me right back to the center. And I ended up right back in the same situation—going home with a foster family."

The foster family turned out to be better than she expected, Athena says.

"They weren't bad at all," she shrugs. "Shannon, the mom, got mad one time and threw an iron at me, but that was pretty much as bad as it ever was. She and her husband were pretty cool. There was me and Dana, this other foster kid. And then they had their own small kids. They'd let me and Dana go out at night and get high—they didn't have a problem with it.

"The thing that got me taken out of there was that Shannon ran this day care out of her home. And she had me and Dana staying home pretty much all the time taking care of kids instead of going to school. I guess I could have forced the issue and demanded to go. But hey—why?" she laughs. "Anyway, my social worker came around one day and saw what was going on. So I got taken out."

BACK TO MARYLAND

Athena told her social worker that since her mother did not want her, she had no reason to stay in Minnesota. She refused to be placed in any other foster families.

"I asked to go back home—to Maryland," she says. "It seems funny, maybe, because of the beatings and everything—but like the saying goes, 'The devil you know is better than the devil you

Although damaged, Athena's internal strength seems not to have left her. She has managed to survive her parents' terrible beatings, abandonment, foster homes, and shelters.

don't.' I knew what to expect at my dad's. I could survive there, I figured. It was better than going to someplace strange and starting over again. So I said that my dad would take me or he wouldn't take me, but either way, I'm not staying here anymore.

"So my dad did take me. I was fifteen and spent a pretty depressing summer back in Maryland. Part of the trouble, looking back, is that Adam seemed so angry with me. I guess in his mind, when I'd left two years ago, I was abandoning him, just like my mom did. So I guess he had a right to be angry. But it depressed me since he was the one guy that I used to have a bond with.

"My dad and my stepmother, Helen, had a little girl named Megan. She was so cool—I just loved her. But my dad didn't let me pick her up or anything. It was so weird. I think it had to do with my being gay. See, I'd known I was gay for a long time. In fact, when I'd been in that treatment facility, I'd called my dad and Helen and come out to them. It didn't seem like it really upset my dad then—Adam told me later my dad figured it was just my way of rebelling—like it was a phase."

"No One Had Ever Stood Up for Me and Adam"

"I felt bad being sort of segregated from Megan. I also noticed some weird dynamics going on between my dad and Helen. He was hitting her, too—at least slapping her around. He'd be mean to her sometimes and drag her off to their room, and she'd come back later crying. She'd go out for a walk—be gone about a half hour. Then she'd come home and be real quiet."

Athena reflects on this for a while, just sitting still and thinking.

"You know, I should make something real clear," she says. "Helen really did sort of try in her own way to get my dad to back off hitting us. See, at first when she married my dad, she didn't understand how it was. I think maybe she just figured he was spanking us or something. I remember how she used to get mad at me and Adam for something—when someone would raise up their arm, the two of us would flinch. She'd get embarrassed if we did that when we were out someplace. She'd say, 'Shame on you two— you'd think you were getting beat! What will people think?'

"Anyway, one time she walked in on me and Adam in the bathroom; we used to compare the welts and bruises on our backs and stuff. This was before I got sent to treatment. Anyway, she walked in and was really shocked at the stuff on our bodies. She got this funny look on her face and kind of went, 'Ohhh!' After that, she didn't really tell my dad when we'd do something wrong. In her own way, she was trying to stick up for us.

"I only know of one time when he slugged Megan," says Athena. We were sitting at the dinner table, all of us. Megan had this habit of sucking on her two middle fingers, and my dad

90

hated it. Anyhow, she did that, and he backhanded her—hard. Oh, Helen got so mad! She slugged him back! She said, 'You might do that to your own kids, but you're not going to do it to mine—we'll leave!'"

Athena smiles, a little sadly. "I remember feeling like, 'Yeah! Someone stood up to him, finally.' But also I guess I felt a little jealous that no one had ever stood up for me and Adam."

"BACK AND FORTH"

Athena spent most of that summer drinking and using drugs—and withdrawing more and more. At the end of the summer, Helen discovered Athena in the middle of overdosing.

"I got sent to the hospital and then to a psych ward," she says. "I went to another treatment facility and then came back up to Minnesota. It was like pinball—back and forth. I didn't have any expectations this time—I worked out a deal with my mom and my stepfather where I'd work, go to school, and pay rent.

"For a while it worked okay. I stayed out of their way. I took a course to become a nursing assistant—you don't have to have a diploma or anything for that. I got a job in a long-term care facility, just taking vital signs and giving baths. And I went to school. Every once in a while my mom or stepfather would go off on me, but they drank a lot, and I stayed out of sight.

"Things blew up after parent-teacher conferences at my high school. My mom went. One of the teachers made the suggestion to her that she needed to be a more responsible parent."

Athena rolls her eyes. "Man, you don't want to be making suggestions about parenting to my mom—she hates it. See, she gets upset when people accuse her of not being a good mother. She says, 'I am a good mother.' And then she can never think of anything else to say, like to back that up. So she gets frustrated.

"Anyhow, that's what happened. She got real rowdy during the conferences, and the vice principal had to tell her to leave. She was screaming, yelling, being really awful. I wasn't there, but I've seen it a million times."

A BAD BEATING

Athena came home from work that afternoon, not realizing what had happened at the high school. When she walked in the door, her mother and stepfather were waiting for her.

"To be blunt, they beat the crap out of me," she says, shrugging. "The two of them together, one holding me, the other kicking. I got kicked in the back, the head. I had some fingernail scratches or something from my forehead all the way down my scalp. Blood was coming down my face, and I didn't know where it was coming from.

"I just ran out of there, and luckily they didn't follow. I ran to my friend Sheena—she works at a grocery store down the street. I asked if I could go to her house and ice myself up, stop the bleeding. But it so happened that Sheena's foster mom was there, and she saw me. She's nice—she's a mandated reporter, which meant that she *had* to report the abuse to the police."

Athena was taken to the police station, where photographers took pictures of her wounds.

"I finally got to look in the mirror," she says. "I looked so ugly! My eyes were swollen under here, and my ear was all black. Those horrible scratches were all swollen and bloody. I had a handprint across my face from getting hit so hard. My back had old bruises, too—knuckle prints and stuff. The cops made me strip down so they could take lots of pictures. Then I went to intake at child protection, where they did all that stuff all over again. They finally let me go to a shelter—and I didn't even go outside for like five days. Man, I looked awful," she says, shaking her head.

OUTED

Athena was placed in another foster family—this time with a husband and wife who were police officers. Did she like them? Athena makes a face and shakes her head vigorously.

"Not at all," she says. "One of the foster kids there, a girl a little younger than me, figured out I was queer. I mean, I wasn't out to anyone but my parents, so she had no way of knowing. This girl used to spit at me and call me 'dyke,' stuff like that.

"Anyway, I had a journal that I kept—just wrote my personal thoughts, things I was thinking about—and she must have gotten ahold of it. When I came home from work one day no one would talk to me! It was like I was invisible. I went to the parents and said, 'Jim, Pam, what's going on? Why is everyone looking at me all dirty?'

"So they say, 'We hear that you're gay.' I was so shocked! I thought, what do you mean, you *hear* that I'm gay? Anyway, this girl had told a big lie, told them that I'd threatened her sexually—

Athena relaxes with her friend Nicole. At seventeen, Athena was given the choice to live on her own, though she did not really know how she was going to do it.

that was *so* not true—and they believed her! They said, 'How dare you bring this filth into our house.' So that was that. They didn't want me—I'd been outed, and by a real jerk. So they told me to leave. I was so angry at how they treated me, I can't even tell you."

Athena got in touch with her social worker, who told her that the courts were not going to fight very hard to place her anywhere. She was seventeen, he said, and how did she feel about being on her own?

"I thought, why not?" she says. "I felt like I'd be better off on my own than with any of the adults I'd met so far, including my mother, my father, and all the rest of them. So the court released custody of me, and I was on my own."

Athena grins. "It was sort of scary but sort of exciting, I guess," she says. "I couldn't be termed a runaway anymore—no worrying about being picked up by child protection or other cops."

A THROWAWAY

While the term *runaway* no longer fit, Athena says that *throwaway* became more appropriate.

"Throwaways are kids who are out on the street because nobody wants them," she says. "Their parents don't have any interest in getting them back, so they stay on the streets. That's what most of the homeless kids are, anyway—not that many are runaways.

"Runaways usually go home after a couple weeks; they hardly ever last longer than a month. They leave home because they're mad, and they want some attention from their parents, and they're pretty sure they'll get it. In a way, those kids are luckier because they've got more options. With throwaways, it's like we know we're really not wanted, not welcome.

"So anyway, once I was on my own, I didn't really have much of a plan. I'd heard of this center for gay and lesbian kids over in Minneapolis. I called them up, got directions, and went over there. When I got there, I told myself, 'Okay, now's your chance to make some friends.' So I did."

In talking to the teens at the center, Athena discovered that the majority of them were homeless—in one sense or another.

"It's not like they were all staying in shelters," she says, "but they didn't have homes. Lots didn't get along with parents, and had been kicked out. Some slept outside, some were couch crashers. The center didn't open until afternoon; it wasn't a place to eat or sleep, just somewhere kids could be themselves, just relax. I spent a lot of time there."

LEARNING THE ROPES

Athena says that most of what she learned about surviving as a homeless person she learned from friends she met at the center—especially Jim and Dizzy.

"Jim was the best couch crasher I ever knew," she smiles. "He knew so many people, and everybody liked him. If anyone could get his hands on a couch for the night, or talk someone into letting him sleep over, it was Jim. And Dizzy was remarkable, too. Dizzy is someone that people sometimes labeled 'slow,' but that's just because of the way he talks. His words come out slow, but his mind is *so* fast! Dizzy is so aware of his surroundings (a very important

Athena stands under the bridge that used to be a frequent squatting place: "It's really, really dangerous. You always want to have somebody up so's they can watch your back when you're sleeping."

homeless skill) that he knows what's going on behind his back with-out even turning around. He's eighteen, I guess—a year younger than me. Dizzy's been on his own since he was fourteen, I think.

"Number one rule is that you never squat alone. [Squatting is homeless jargon for sleeping in a park, in an abandoned building, or under a bridge—anywhere homeless people know they can sleep for a few hours.] It's really, really dangerous. You always want to have somebody up so's they can watch your back when you're sleeping. And then you help them out the same way.

"Like under a bridge, you can hear people around you, even if you can't always see them. You can hear them coughing or getting up to pee or something. You've just got to listen to the noises, make sure nobody's getting threatened. In a group, you're less likely to get raped, mugged, or jumped."

Athena says that the people who prey on homeless people are not necessarily other homeless people.

"I think that's wrong," she says. "Maybe the police or the city officials would like to have people believe that because then they can blame homeless people for one more of society's ills. But the truth is, lots of bad guys out there are messing with homeless peo-ple. Some are tough guys, just looking for someone vulnerable. Some are even *cops*—I've seen police officers start beating on homeless kids for no reason.

"There's ways cities have of hassling homeless people, too," she adds. "Cops can let their dogs loose just to scare people. Or some-times they just set the sprinklers up so that you can't find a place to stay dry at night."

WHAT YOU NEED IF YOU'RE HOMELESS

What has she learned from living on the streets? Athena smiles, taking out her army-green backpack, which she'd put under her chair.

"*This* is what you need," she crows. "It's the first thing any homeless person needs—it's a must. A good sturdy bag, like this one. See," she says, pointing, "mine is decorated with all kinds of things I've been given or have found. I've got a sticker from a ska band I really like, another one here—this one's my favorite—it's an oxymoron. It says, "I HATE JUDGMENTAL PEOPLE.""

Athena holds up the backpack, showing off its other side. "Here's a rainbow badge I found, and a sticker against police bru-

Athena is proud of her bag and the survival equipment it carries: "You always carry duct tape and a wrench. The duct tape—man, it's crucial!"

tality. And inside I've got my case of insulin and my syringes and a change of clothes—I told you I still feel homeless!

"And here—you *always* carry duct tape and a wrench. The duct tape—man, it's crucial! It keeps your clothes together, your pants up, your boots from leaking. And the wrench is important for getting into places, like a squat, or for a weapon if someone tries to mess with you. My friends call things like that 'smileys.' I guess because you smile confidently if you've got one. Dizzy never had a wrench, he carried a long bike chain with a big lock on it. He had no bike, but he could whip the chain at somebody if he was in trouble. That was his smiley."

When winter comes and no couches can be found for crashing, Athena found that garbage bags—big ones—were valuable.

"We'd wrap them around ourselves and dig down deep in the snow," she says. "That's good for insulation. Or sometimes you can get real lucky at the Salvation Army and find a sleeping bag—and you can pile three people in it. Or some homeless kids have dogs just so they can cuddle up with them at night. The only thing hard about that is feeding him—it's expensive. If you're panhandling, it's usually hard just to get enough for feeding yourself one meal, you know?"

"I DON'T THINK TOO MANY PEOPLE REALLY CARE"

Athena bristles at the idea that the homeless problem among teenagers is exaggerated.

"I've heard people say, 'There can't be *that* many homeless kids—they wouldn't stay in this climate very long!' That's not true!" she says vehemently. "Sure, some kids get on a train and head out West in the fall when the weather changes, but lots and lots stay here. And there are only like fifty-four shelter beds in this city—only fifty-four allotted to teenagers! There are so many more—hundreds more than that. They're sleeping in the park, sleeping in the warehouses and closed-up theaters, they're under the bridges. And I don't think too many people really care. If this city cared, kids wouldn't be freezing outside all winter long.

"During the day there are more choices, of course. You can go to the library and read. Dizzy and Jim and I used to go to Barnes and Noble downtown—it was so comfortable; they've got these great chairs. We'd stick out like sore thumbs from their other customers, but the people were pretty cool. We'd read poetry—Emily Dickinson and stuff like that. That's a pretty good memory."

There are plenty of memories that aren't so good, however, especially those of her increasing drug use.

"I was using my insulin syringes for shooting up glass—crystal meth. It's a pure form of speed, comes in little rock crystals. You just inject it in a vein, like shooting up heroin. My needles are small, so they were good for that, so my veins didn't get all collapsed."

FOR "THREE HOTS AND A COT"

She shows a mark on the inside of her elbow—one on each arm.

"See," she says, pointing to a little round mark, "there's where I used to shoot up. Sometimes I'd do it between my toes. I'll tell you something—with glass I wouldn't feel as much being homeless. I didn't feel the cold as bad. And I could forget how hungry I was— sometimes, actually, I'd forget to eat. And I wasn't as afraid.

Athena prepares to give herself an insulin shot. She used to use her insulin needles for drugs: "My needles are small, so they were good for that."

"Sometimes me and this guy named Max would go prostituting just to earn some money," she says in a very small voice. "And we'd watch each other, make sure we were okay. I'd watch the cars he got in, he'd do the same for me. And the glass would help—I could never have done that stuff sober.

"The other thing I remember, that wasn't so nice, was how hard it was to get arrested when we wanted to—when we just couldn't face another night outside. We'd rather go to jail or some facility than squat outside in the snow. We'd call it 'three hots and a cot.' But you know, when you want to get arrested, you can't! I remember lying on the sidewalk in the park, right in front of a cop, and he wouldn't arrest me. And once I was drinking, right in front of a cop. I said, 'Look, I'm drinking here in the park.' He just said, 'Okay, well, don't do that again.' Sometimes you just can't win.

"A couple of times I even skipped my insulin shots on purpose. Usually I'm really good about taking them—I was on medical assistance and could get supplies just by showing my card at the drugstore. But if I skip two shots, I get real sick and have to go to the hospital. I wear this ID bracelet, so they know just what to do. But God, the lengths I used to go just to eat, just to stay warm."

JANE AND THE "KICK-ASS" NUNS

Her homeless days came to an end rather suddenly, Athena says. Her drug use was out of hand, and she was constantly ill.

"I knew I couldn't go through the cold weather again," she says. "I remembered this one special ed teacher I'd had in high school—her name was Jane. She was so nice; she knew I had troubles back then. When I'd left the class she told me that I should call her if I ever needed anything. She was sort of well-known for going above and beyond the call of duty, you know? Like there was this one kid, Cory—he's in jail in another state—and she writes to him all the time.

"So anyway, I decided I'd hold her to it. I called her; told her I was high, but when I was sober I hated myself. I looked awful from shooting up all the time. I was so, so thin, and my eyes were all sunken back; my skin was awful. I looked in the mirror and it made me so sad. I told her that I was pale, addicted, and I couldn't stop—I couldn't even get out of bed without shooting up.

"She asked me if I really, really wanted to quit. I told her yeah, I did. So she told me to come over to her house. So I went through drug withdrawal right there, with her. The first week I didn't even get out of bed! I was so sick I couldn't move. And I had night sweats—we had to change my sheets in the middle of the night. The pillowcases just stunk! I just reeked, and I was crabby, too. But she put up with me.

"The next week I felt a little better. I tried things like walking downstairs. I started really feeling like I wasn't going to die after all. Anyway, Jane had a friend who knew about this place called Rose Center, run by nuns. It's like a place for women to get back on their feet—young women like me. Lots have been in abusive situations or homeless."

Athena smiles. "And these were not your ordinary nuns—at least not the kind I'm used to. They were kind and helpful and nonjudgmental. I was out with them, and they didn't have a problem. They were great—really kick-ass.

"I lived at the center for about six months. I didn't use any drugs at all. I wasn't going to school, but I got a job when I was there at a preschool—I was a child care aid. That was about thirty-eight hours a week."

The rules at the center were rigid, but Athena says she had no trouble obeying them.

"It was no drugs, no drinking, no boys staying over," she says. "Like falling off a log for me; it was easy. I do admit I had a couple of homeless friends I snuck in. Stuck them in a dress and smuggled them in on cold nights. They were my friends; what could I do? But everything went fine, just fine."

"My Life Is So Different"

After spending six months there, Athena was ready to become a little more independent, and the Host Home program seemed like a good idea. She moved in with Ed a few weeks ago.

"I admit I'm more comfortable with kids my own age—I'm used to that," she says. "When I go over to my friend's house—we squeeze like fifteen in there, and it feels like the old days, just being with lots of people at once. But I'll get used to things at Ed's. It will just take time.

"I don't like to look ahead or make plans. I'd never do that! I mean, the last thing I want to do is set myself up for disappointment. My life is so different from the way I'd hoped it would be, way back when I was little. If there's one thing I've learned, it's not to predict the future.

Athena plays her guitar in the peacefulness of Ed's home. She takes it one day at a time, working job to job, unable to trust in a stable future.

"As far as work goes, I kind of take it step by step. I'm more into doing projects now—do a job, wait until the money runs out, and then get another one. Now I'm reading grant proposals for the Department of Health. I get like three hundred dollars for a project like that. Also, there's a position coming open soon at the gay and lesbian center. I've got my résumé—such as it is—in order. It doesn't look like much on the education end since I haven't finished high school or even gotten my GED. But experience-wise I'd be pretty good. I'd be a familiar face to a lot of the kids who come in but not so close to them that I'd cross the line. I don't want to be back homeless or doing drugs anymore. That's behind me."

What about her family? Athena says she has no interest in them.

"I care a lot about my brother," she says. "I went down to see him graduate from high school last spring. Actually, except for that one summer when he was sort of mad at me, we've stayed really close. He has his own problems—he's a really angry kid. I know he comes by that honestly!

"But inside he's really a very sweet guy. When I was back this spring, the family was actually very harsh on me, but Adam kind of put them in check—he really stuck up for me. He actually went with me to the gay pride weekend down there! And oh, did my dad ream him out—'What are doing going down there with a bunch of faggots; what's the matter with you?' Adam just said, 'I went to support Athena. She's gay and we all know it—and you should be down there, too.' It was so cool!" Athena says, smiling. "I thought to myself—I *do* have someone in this family who cares."

Epilogue

In the time since these four teens were interviewed, some aspects of their lives have changed. Alvin was suspended from school just three days before summer vacation started. He had gotten into a fight with another student, and the principal was unyielding. Alvin says he didn't care because he didn't like school all that much anyway.

Nina, as well as her group of friends, are no longer at the shelter. No one has seen them—or Nina's mother, for that matter. One young man at the shelter said he's heard a rumor that Nina moved to Wisconsin, but he's not sure if that is true.

Athena is doing well. She and her housemate Ed are getting along better; she is becoming more comfortable with the situation, she says. She is proud that she and Ed recently appeared on a local news segment about the Host Home project.

Andre, like Nina, seems to have disappeared. His manager at McDonald's says he hasn't seen him in months, and that seems funny to him. "Andre never even picked up his last check," he says, "and that doesn't make sense—I know he could use the money!"

Ways You Can Get Involved

THE FOLLOWING ORGANIZATIONS CAN BE CONTACTED FOR MORE INFORMATION ABOUT HOMELESS TEENS.

National Alliance to End Homelessness
1518 K St. NW
Washington, DC 20005

This organization works to educate communities about the ways they can battle homelessness, from improving drug and substance abuse agencies to increasing the amount of available low-income housing.

National Coalition for the Homeless
1439 Rhode Island Ave. NW
Washington, DC 20005

This coalition offers legislative information for homeless families, and it can also direct families to the nearest available shelter.

National Low Income Housing Coalition
1012 14th St. NW
Washington, DC 20005

This coalition lobbies for more and better-quality affordable housing. It also provides educational services.

Youth and Child Resource Net
267 Lester Ave., Suite 104
Oakland, CA 94606

This organization helps runaways get off the streets and assists them in finding help for alcohol and other substance addictions.

For Further Reading

Jeffrey Artenstein, *Runaways*. New York: Tom Doherty, 1990.
A readable collection of firsthand accounts of street kids in
Hollywood.

Eleanor H. Ayer, *Homeless Children*. San Diego: Lucent Books, 1997.
An in-depth look at homeless children, many of whom are runaways.

Margaret O. Hyde, *The Homeless: Profiling the Problem*. Hillside, NJ:
Enslow, 1989. Excellent section on throwaways.

Matthew Kraljic, ed., *The Homeless Problem*. New York: H. W. Wil-
son, 1992. Some excellent firsthand accounts of being homeless
in a large city.

Charles A. Kroloff, *Fifty-Four Ways You Can Help the Homeless*.
West Orange, NJ: Behrman House, 1993. Some practical ways
that people can fight poverty and homelessness in their communities.

Milton Meltzer, *Poverty in America*. New York: William Morrow,
1986. Excellent index; good information on women and homelessness.

Index

ABOUT THE AUTHOR

Gail B. Stewart is the author of more than eighty books for children and young adults. She lives in Minneapolis, Minnesota, with her husband, Carl, and their sons, Ted, Elliot, and Flynn. When she is not writing, she spends her time reading, walking, and watching her sons play soccer.

Although she has enjoyed working on each of her books, she says that *The Other America* series has been especially gratifying. "So many of my past books have involved extensive research," she says, "but most of it has been library work—journals, magazines, books. But for these books, the main research has been very human. Spending the day with a little girl who has AIDS, or having lunch in a soup kitchen with a homeless man—these kinds of things give you insight that a library alone just can't match."

Stewart hopes that readers of this series will experience some of the same insights—perhaps even being motivated to use some of the suggestions at the end of each book to become involved with someone of the Other America.

About the Photographer

Carl Franzén is a writer/designer who enjoys using the camera to tell a story. He works out of his home in Minneapolis where he lives with his wife, three boys, two dogs, and one cat. For lots of fun, camaraderie, and meeting interesting people, he coaches youth soccer and edits a neighborhood newsletter.